Citizen
Shakespeare

CITIZEN
SHAKESPEARE

A Social and Political Portrait

JAMES C. HUMES

Forewords by

Lord Crathorne,
John F. Andrews, *and*
Ronnie Mulryne

Westport, Connecticut
London

Library of Congress Cataloging-in-Publication Data

Humes, James C.
    Citizen Shakespeare : a social and political portrait / James C.
Humes ; forewords by Lord Crathorne, John F. Andrews, Ronnie Mulryne.
      p. cm.
    Includes bibliographical references and index.
    ISBN 0–275–94153–1 (alk. paper)
    1. Shakespeare, William, 1564–1616—Political and social views.
2. Dramatists, English—Early modern, 1500–1700—Biography.
3. Politics and literature—England—History—16th century.
4. Politics and literature—England—History—17th century.
5. Literature and society—England—History—16th century.
6. Literature and society—England—History—17th century.
7. Political plays, English—History and criticism. 8. Social
problems in literature.   I. Title.
PR3017.H86   1993
822.3′3—dc20   92–3365

British Library Cataloguing in Publication Data is available.

Library of Congress Catalog Card Number: 92–3365
ISBN: 0–275–94153–1

First published in 1993

Praeger Publishers, 88 Post Road West, Westport, CT 06881
An imprint of Greenwood Publishing Group, Inc.

Printed in the United States of America

The paper used in this book complies with the
Permanent Paper Standard issued by the National
Information Standards Organization (Z39.48–1984).

10 9 8 7 6 5 4 3 2 1

To O. B. Hardison, Jr., scholar, prophet, and lover of the English language.
His vision and incandescent spirit shaped the Folger Shakespeare Library and made Shakespeare a continuing presence in our nation's capital, to influence the minds of future generations.

a rarer spirit never
Did steer humanity: but you, gods, will give us
Some faults to make us men.

Antony and Cleopatra

There is a history in all men's lives,
Figuring the nature of the times decreased;
The which observed, a man may prophesy,
With a near aim, of the main chance of things.

II Henry IV

Contents

Foreword

We live in a time of rapid change and so did Shakespeare. Shakespeare's writings reflect many of those changes. He greatly extended the English vocabulary, colloquializing in much the same manner as our modern entertainment business is doing. Shakespeare would surely have found his way to Hollywood if he were alive today.

The Shakespearean scholar, A. L. Rowse, in a recent interview, summed up the reason why Shakespeare is as relevant today as he was to his contemporaries. "William Shakespeare has the way of absolutely piercing right through your heart. The whole of life is in him, really."

James Humes, by placing Shakespeare in the context of his own time, increases our understanding of both the man and his plays. A project that will have a similar effect is the rebuilding of Shakespeare's Globe Theatre, very close to the site of the original, on the south bank of the Thames. The first Globe stood for only 14 years, from 1599 to 1613, when it was burnt down during a performance of *Henry VIII*. Such was its popularity that it was quickly replaced and operated until it was shut down by Oliver Cromwell and the Puritans in 1642. The catalyst behind the rebuilding project, 400 years later, is the actor and producer Sam Wanamaker; soon we will be able to see Shakespeare's plays in their original setting and context.

The Elizabethans built the first permanent theaters and as a result actors ceased to be "rogues, vagabonds, and sturdy beggars" and no longer had to use public inn-yards, marketplaces, and churchyards.

The first of these permanent theaters was built by James Burbage in 1576, when Shakespeare was a boy, and was simply called "The Theatre."

The first Globe is of special interest because, for the very first time, the actors were shareholders and Shakespeare's 10 percent share was to make him a rich man. This did not mean that the system of patronage of actors and writers by the Court and gentry disappeared. My direct ancestor, the Earl of Southampton, was the first person who recognized Shakespeare's genius and the playwright dedicated his first published poems to him. Southampton's payment of £1,000 (one million dollars today) provided the investment Shakespeare needed to establish himself as a property owner in Stratford. Southampton devoted much of his energies to the new colony in Virginia. He encouraged Shakespeare to write his last great play, *The Tempest*, as a result of his experiences in the "brave new world."

Elizabethan theater was the most popular of all time and it is said that 25 percent of the population of London came to see Shakespeare's plays, paying the penny entrance—or tuppence, if they wished to have a seat.

Shakespeare came closer than any playwright has done to incorporate the sacred and profane; the serious and ridiculous, the romantic and satirical, the gentle and rough, the earthy and pure. The Globe was indeed well-named as Shakespeare transported his audiences from the taverns of Cheapside to the "vasty fields of France" and beyond and enabled them to "travel" without help of scenery or elaborate props, relying on the skillful use of language. In *Henry V*, Shakespeare explains how he expected his audience to react "within this wooden O" and makes a request in the prologue:

> Think when we talk of horses that you see them
> Printing their proud hoofs i' the receiving earth;
> For 'tis your thoughts that now must deck our kings,
> Carry them here and there, jumping o'er times,
> Turning the accomplishment of many years
> Into an hour-glass.

This real participation and use of imagination by the audience is different from many of our experiences in the theatre now. The rebuilt Globe will ensure that we will again see Shakespeare's plays in their context and James Humes's book helps us do the same.

Shakespeare was constantly breaking new ground. He used the past as a means of exploring human nature and the human spirit. He reveals man to himself through his infinite understanding of mankind and as a result has made our future better.

Lord Crathorne

Foreword

There are probably more courageous things a person can do than to attempt a life of Shakespeare. But there can't be many. Anyone who has ever contemplated the problem of extracting a coherent story from the scant material available for such an undertaking can see why the task has proved too daunting for most of the scholars who have devoted careers to the study of Shakespeare's works and the social, political, and artistic contexts that conditioned the production of those works.

In our era the biographer who has sifted the evidence most thoroughly has been Sam Schoenbaum, an authority so meticulous and judicious in his methods that few have dared to question even the conclusion he admits to holding tentatively. It is true that a handful of recent analyses have taken issue with Schoenbaum's approaches to particular aspects of Shakespeare's professional development; I think of Russell Fraser's book about the poet's youth, for example, or Ernst Honigmann's investigation of the so-called "lost years" (a seven-year period for which we have no indisputuable records of the future playwright's whereabouts), or Leeds Barroll's assessment of the effect that outbreaks of the plague may have had on the last decade of Shakespeare's dramatic output. But so far—and no doubt for good reason—no one has come forward with a grand synthesis to supersede such Schoenbaum classics as *Shakespeare's Lives* and *William Shakespeare: A Documentary Life*.

The consequence is that we remain without a portrayal of the playwright that can satisfy everybody's curiosity. On the one hand we have a small shelf of books and articles that focus on the little that can be proven about

Shakespeare the man and all the people who came in contact with him. By their nature these studies are like Schoenbaum's: they stick as closely as possible to "the facts, ma'am," and they eschew unanchored speculation about how those facts fit into larger patterns of narrative that might plausibly account for them. On the other hand we have a vast library of books and articles about the poems and plays of Shakespeare the writer and theater professional. For the most part, these studies avoid biographical issues: they stick as closely as possible to another set of "facts." What we lack is a volume that draws these disparate strands of material together and relates them to a more general survey of Tudor-Stuart England and its position in the history of early modern Europe.

As Richmond Crinkley put it several years ago, what gnaws at us—and what drives a few to the hypothesis that someone else must have written the world's most influential literature and drama—is "the absence," in most interpretations of William Shakespeare, "of a life with anybody living in it."

In the chapters that follow, James Humes endeavors to confront that void. Emboldened by the indomitable spirit of the late O. B. Hardison, Jr., a Renaissance man who never met a challenge he didn't like, Mr. Humes essays to present a Shakespeare who makes sense to the modern reader and playgoer: a poet who would have understood, and have been stimulated by, the trials of twentieth-century culture because he was one of the first to recognize that his own culture was informed by many of the pressures we now take for granted. Mr. Humes brings unique credentials to what he clearly regards as a labor of love, and it gives me great pleasure to support his cause with this humble foreword.

John F. Andrews
Editor of *The Guild Shakespeare*

Foreword

"He was not of an age, but for all time." Ben Jonson's familiar words from the verses for the Shakespeare Folio of 1623 have been echoed in numerous assessments of the great dramatist's work over the four centuries that separate his time from ours. The work of distinguished biographers such as E. K. Chambers, Samuel Schoenbaum, M. M. Reese, and E. A. J. Honigmann has ensured that we know what there is to be known about the facts of his life, few though these are. Historians and cultural historians, including the same scholars, have related the facts to the social and political circumstances of Shakespeare's day and have helped us to see how the circumstances shaped the plays and the plays reflected and influenced the circumstances. Critics of all persuasions have made the plays their own, and have helped to make them ours. Theaters have continued the unbroken tradition of performance down the centuries, renewing the plays in the idiom of each successive generation. The great scholarly collections, as the dedication to the present study acknowledges, have played their central part in making the plays and their literary and theatrical milieu continuously accessible: the Folger Shakespeare Library in Washington, D.C., and its former director O. B. Hardison, Jr., have by their generosity helped to provide the intellectual and practical circumstances in which the study of Shakespeare and his work could be fruitfully pursued. In all these ways, and more, the permanence of Shakespeare in our culture has been ensured: he has been proved to be, till now and for the foreseeable future, not for an age but for all time.

Yet the place of Shakespeare in our culture is not a simple topic and has not been, and is not, without controversy. This is not just a matter of the disintegrators and perpetrators of heresy. The intellectual snobbery of the Baconians and the followers of the Earl of Oxford, unable to credit a simple country-educated writer with the unbounded genius of Shakespeare, has been dismissed by the great majority of scholars, and recently by formal hearings before distinguished panels of lawyers in both the United States and Britain. The plays of Shakespeare were beyond reasonable doubt written by the man born in 1564 in Stratford-upon-Avon and baptized in Holy Trinity Church. Much more difficult is the question of who this man was, in terms of the views he held, the people and the politics he admired, and the interaction of his mind with the issues of his day. More difficult still is to maintain a scholarly distinction, while admitting its ultimate impossibility, between the man who was Shakespeare and what we make of him. Those who pine for a value-free biography of Shakespeare, like those who pine for value-free interpretations of his plays, on the stage or in studies, are following an illusion. It is the penalty as well as the reward of Shakespeare's permanence that we must continuously remake him if he is to be a living presence in our culture. Thus we shall have feminist, materialist, and subversive Shakespeares, as well as Shakespeares who are moralist, integrative, and politically orthodox. Hence the justification for each new biography; it is ourselves that we remake. The challenge and the responsibility is to undertake this remaking with scrupulous regard for what is known or can be convincingly inferred about the writer and his time, while remaining aware of, though not apologetic over, our own interests, prejudices, and biases. The discipline of biography, and the reward for its reader, lies in this two-way testing of ourselves against the mind of the biography's subject and the *mentalité* of his time. Shakespeare presents the biographer with what is surely the most inviting and the most daunting challenge of all: the most capacious mind and the richest period in our history, both still variously and potently alive in our own time.

Mr. Humes is very well placed to take the double view of Shakespeare, intimate but detached, that biography demands. American scholars have made outstanding contributions to Shakespeare study, perhaps in part because of the perceptible cultural distance between their civilization and his. Yet Mr. Humes, as president of the Winston Churchill Institute in Washington, D.C., makes clear the strong ties that bind the two nations together. Moreover, Mr. Humes is a descendant of the Sir George Hume who was both a favorite of King James I of England and VI of Scotland, and a lover of theater. The genetic relationship, and the community of interest, must have drawn Mr. Humes toward his formidable task. But perhaps the most evident tie of all lies in Mr. Humes's notable experience as adviser and speechwriter to presidents of the United States: the values and commitments this work entailed are everywhere apparent in the strong attention Mr. Humes pays to the politics of Shakespeare's life and work, and the conclusions he draws. The self that Mr. Humes remakes in this biography should be of compelling interest not only to students of Shakespeare but to all of us alive to the supreme importance of American political ideas in today's world.

Ronnie Mulryne
Professor of English and
Chairman of the Graduate School of Renaissance Studies
University of Warwick, U.K.

Acknowledgments

But for my daughter Rachel, this biography of Shakespeare would never have been written. Her interest rekindled a love of the Bard begun in my schooldays. Together we have seen a score of plays. Her activity in the Shakespeare Society at Wellesley College spurred my own research.

I am indebted to Carol Williams, a trustee of St. Agnes School, who invited me to give the first presentation of my Shakespeare talk. The enthusiastic reception to these talks prompted me to begin this biography.

I am also grateful for the encouragement of Marifrancis Hardison, the widow of O. B. Hardison, Jr. She read my manuscript and offered editorial suggestions. As did her husband, Mrs. Hardison cherishes the English sentence as one of the beauties of God's creation.

Another Shakespeare scholar who read my manuscript was my friend, the poet Robert McQuilken, whose enthusiasm about my biographical insights was a source of inspiration. I also appreciated the invitation to speak to Miss Porter's, the school at which he is head of the English Department.

Others who read my manuscript during its various renditions include Col. Ray Tyrrell; Priscilla Ryan, who runs the Arts Center in Eagles Mere, Pennsylvania; Susie Brant; Donald Whitehead; Peter Van Roijen; and Robert Bland Smith, who first introduced me to O. B. Hardison.

Another who encouraged me to write the biography was Hugh Bullock, the head of the Society of the Pilgrims. As was his late wife Marie, a poet, he is a lover of the English language.

I was honored by the English Speaking Union's invitation to speak at their international meeting at Ottawa, as well as at branch meetings in Philadelphia; Syracuse; Wilmington; and State College, Pennsylvania.

Anyone who has studied Shakespeare will echo my gratitude to the staff of the Folger Shakespeare Library for its ample facilities for research on the world's greatest poet.

My appreciation to Lourdes Z. Monson for her typing assistance.

And my special thanks to Robyn Train, the librarian of the Union League for reading the page proofs.

Finally, I am indebted to Dr. Hall Todd, my friend and probably the most erudite man I know, for his wise suggestions and counsel.

Introduction

A couple of decades ago when I was a White House speech writer, I met O. B. Hardison, Jr., the director of the Folger Shakespeare Library. On subsequent occasions, over tea in his oriental-carpeted and wood-paneled office of the library, we talked about Shakespeare and his enduring influence, which had honed the eloquence of such statesmen as Abraham Lincoln and Winston Churchill. Hardison's soft North Carolina drawl did not disguise his contagious passion for Shakespeare, or mute the power of Shakespeare's poetry. Yet Hardison's range of interests encompassed far more than Elizabethan England, as his last book, *Disappearing through the Skylight*, attests.[1]

I remember his telling me, around the time of the moon landing, that the computer would revolutionize knowledge, just as the printing press had for Renaissance Britain. I was at that time working on a speech book entitled *Instant Eloquence*,[2] and he suggested that I write about Shakespeare someday—not a scholarly tome, but rather an interpretive piece—to encourage students to reach toward the joys of Shakespeare. When I replied that I thought scholars knew little about Shakespeare's life, Hardison answered that enough was known to realize that Shakespeare, as Ben Jonson had said, was "not of an age but for all time."

Hardison also thought that my vantage point as a speech writer in the White House would give me insight about Shakespeare, who had a ringside seat at Court. I had told him that the most memorized speech in the world was that of Mark Antony in *Julius Caesar*. This led us to a discussion of the scores of other political orations that Shakespeare penned. Shakespeare, who had read Machiavelli, was just as keen a student of statecraft. In his chronicles and tragedies, Shakespeare unmasked the public faces of rulers to reveal the private persons, etching the lines of conflict and tension in officers of state. As a speech writer for presidents, I was witness to the workings of such inner drives, and I helped to mold the public image, or as Shakespeare wrote, "to frame a face to fit the occasion." Perhaps my experience as a politician turned writer might bring a new and different look at Shakespeare, through a prism both historical and political.

I reflected on that advice, and on the experiences that drew me to Shakespeare. The first teacher to excite my interest in the Bard had been Paul Chancellor, who taught an experimental humanities course when I was a sixth former at the Hill School in Pottstown, Pennsylvania.

With Chancellor's help, I won an English Speaking Union scholarship to a British public school. There I played the roles, first of Sir Toby Belch, and then of the Second Gentleman in the coronation scene of *Henry VIII*. The *London Times*, in its review, reported that "the American accent of the Second Gentleman seemed somehow appropriate in this Coronation year [1953]."

Ten years later, as a Pennsylvania legislator, I quoted *Macbeth* to the General Assembly in a speech about the successful passage of an administration tax bill. Shortly thereafter, Gov. William Scranton appointed me to the Pennsylvania Shakespeare Quadricentennial Commission, whose other members included Conrad Richter, Andrew Wyeth, and Pearl Buck. In my acceptance to the governor, I quoted Shakespeare's Benedick, "Will your grace command me any service to the world's end? I will go on the slightest errand" (act 2, scene 1). The governor replied in a terse note, "Methinks you are making 'Much Ado About Nothing'."

The purpose of the commission was to amass a cultural inventory of Shakespeare in Pennsylvania—academicians, actors, and memorabilia for the use of high schools and colleges. From that experience I came away with the belief that even the educated had little understanding of the man, who was a primal force in shaping not only our language but our Western values of human rights and dignity.

The seed planted by Hardison started to take root in 1982. I had just completed a biography of Churchill and was spending the year as a Woodrow Wilson Fellow in the Center for International Scholars, preparing a book on great Presidential addresses. I was again fascinated by the influence Shakespeare had on U.S. presidents. For instance, Lincoln, like Churchill, was familiar with Shakespeare's orations and his truths about man's political nature. The language of Shakespeare haunted both men.

The lives of Churchill and Shakespeare, though stemming from different ends of the social spectrum, are strikingly parallel. Both lacked a university education. Both used the English language as a staircase to fame and fortune. Both were men who answered the need of their time. They are the two greatest Englishmen, and they ennobled the English tongue. Yet despite their titanic achievements, both Shakespeare and Churchill preferred to be buried in the country churchyard of their parents, rather than occupy a niche in Westminster Abbey.

I had the opportunity of hearing Churchill in the House of Commons, and of meeting him once, in May 1953, when he told me, "Study history, study history. In history lie all the secrets of statecraft." My connection with Shakespeare was more tenuous, yet still enough to spur my writing. An ancestor of mine, Sir George Hume, a courtier to James I, was Master of the Wardrobe in 1603. It was he who granted the "red livery" to Shakespeare as a "gentleman of the bed chamber," which enabled Shakespeare to become one of the King's Men.

I divulged that connection to my old friend Lord Crathorne, who replied that his ancestor was the Earl of Southampton, who was Shakespeare's patron and a major investor in the first American colonies. James Crathorne is a trustee of England's oldest theater, the Georgian Theatre Royal in Richmond, and runs the All-Party Arts and Heritage Group in the House of Commons and House of Lords. He has lectured on the history of English theater at the Metropolitan Museum in New York. Crathorne agreed that a new biography would add dimension to the enjoyment of playgoers if it helped them to take the measure of the playwright. In that hope, I dedicate my book to O. B. Hardison, whose development of the Folger Shakespeare Library has preserved and enhanced the English language's greatest treasure.

NOTES

1. O. B. Hardison, Jr., *Disappearing through the Skylight* (New York: Viking, 1989).
2. James C. Humes, *Instant Eloquence* (New York: Harper and Row, 1973).

Citizen
Shakespeare

CHAPTER ONE

A Father's Dream

Cry 'God for [William], England, and Saint George!'

Henry V,
act 3, scene 1

In sixteenth-century England there were few more festive occasions than April 23, which was the feast of Saint George, the patron saint of England. It was a day of national pride and celebration, not unlike the American Fourth of July. Every English village and town staged a procession. Horses pulled carts with statues of Saint George and a papier-mâché dragon, the beast of legend that the martyred Roman centurion had mythically slain. Standard bearers marched holding aloft the English flag, which featured the red cross of St. George on a white field. Richard the Lion-Hearted had designed this English flag three centuries earlier, when he led one of the first crusades to the Holy Land.

So the day of April 23, 1564, found the market center of Stratford in a holiday mood. The Warwickshire community derived its name from the Saxon word for road, *strat*, and the shallow place in the Avon River that allowed horses to *ford* their way across. The town, of hardly more than 2,000, was stretched to its limits as visiting folk from neighboring villages and farms thronged the streets for the feast day celebration. As townspeople proclaimed their toasts to England's patron saint from the windows of the plaster- and wood-framed Tudor shops, the procession wended its merry way along Henley Street, over cobblestones still wet from spring rains.

But in all likelihood, one local tradesman was not out on the streets celebrating with bannock cakes and steins of ale. John Shakespeare was no doubt beside his wife Mary, who was giving birth to their first son after two daughters. Their house on Henley Street, with rush-strewn floors and low ceilings and beams darkening from the open fireplaces, was stocked with the heaps of linen and pewter goblets and silver cutlery that bespoke the comfort of a prospering merchant. The bed of birth where his wife lay was a half-headed frame, with an empty, swaddled rocking cradle awaiting the new infant. Next to the bed was a carved chest, and on the wall above the bed hung a tapestry depicting biblical events.

If John Shakespeare was toasting a soldier, it was probably not the Roman centurion George of Appodocia, but the Norman conqueror William, after whom he named his son. John would christen his son three days later, at the Holy Trinity Church, which stood by the Avon River.[1]

William the Conqueror had established what is now the British royal family line, and John Shakespeare dreamed of beginning his own noble line. But the background of John Shakespeare was far from noble. He was a humble tradesman who could neither read nor write. Yet his trade of making tailor-made gloves for gentlemen put him in contact with the best people of Stratford. John had apprenticed as a whittawer. A whittawer made white leather from the skins of deer, sheep, and goats. The skins, soaked in a solution of alum and salt, were stretched and beaten out with sharp knives until they were soft and pliant. Gloves were an essential item of dress, and not just for keeping hands warm. They were fashionable and expensive. Often richly embroidered or beaded—even jewelled—gloves were badges of rank.

While he cut patterns out of leather in his Henley Street shop, he would hear the hammering of the blacksmithery[2] next door. Later his son would write in *King John*:

> I saw a smith stand with his hammer thus
> The whilst his iron did on the anvil cool
> With open mouth swallowing a tailor's news
> Who with his shears and measure in his hand
> Standing on slippers which his nimble haste
> Had falsely thrust upon contrary feet.

Amid the anvil rings, John might have imagined hearing himself greeted over and over as "Master Shakespeare, Master Shakespeare." Such was the salutation to a gentleman. One day he would no longer answer to just "John."

But he would not be Master Shakespeare, unless he was awarded a coat of arms. John Shakespeare had already designed just how such heraldry would look. A falcon and a spear, with the motto in French, *Non Sans Droit*—"Not without right." The French phrase would reaffirm the justice of his claim. He had asked his lawyer to submit his application to the College of Heralds in London; this was not so much a college, but a court that would hear and rule on such petitions. Money alone could not buy a title, but money together with influence could place a petition in friendly hands.[3] In the new Renaissance England, money was mobility, and for a price a pedigree could be invented, a coat-of-arms granted. Dress and behavior would do the rest.[4]

From the growing profits of his glove shop, John Shakespeare had stashed away some shillings to buy land. To be a gentleman, one first had to own land. John Shakespeare was also acquiring some influence, as he maneuvered his way up in local politics. He had started out as a humble ale taster, but he reached the post of high bailiff. The ale taster and the bread weigher were the lowliest of municipal officials, while the high bailiff was the equivalent of mayor. When he advanced from alderman to high bailiff, he would exchange the alderman's black gown for the bailiff's scarlet robe.

John Shakespeare was an ambitious man. The son of Richard Shakespeare, a tenant farmer in Snitterfield, he had struck out on his own. From laboring in a slaughterhouse, he had advanced to clerking in a glover's shop, with some selling of wool on the side.[5] He had progressed from butcher to shop owner to wool merchant. In later life, Will Shakespeare drew on his memories of his father's wool dealing and put them to comic use in *The Winter's Tale*. The clown in that play is a shepherd's son, and when he first appears he is trying (unsuccessfully) to work out the value of the wool that has just been sheared from his father's flock.

Today, a John Shakespeare would fit right into the local Rotary Club. A hearty fellow with ruddy checks, he would have had a friendly greeting for each of the various artisans. In his day these were the shoemaker, wheelwright, cooper, dyer, butcher, and thatcher. A typical small-town politician, John Shakespeare wanted to be liked and was likeable. Tradesmen, as well as his fellow merchants, did not begrudge the jolly Shakespeare's rapid rise from butcher boy to wool merchant.

The political sense of the future playwright came from his politician father. As high bailiff, John's duties included that of magistrate. In his role as justice of the peace, John Shakespeare would render decisions on tavern brawls, family quarrels, and property squabbles. He would deal out writs of debt and warrants for arrest. Years later his son might have recalled some of those disputes in these words from *Troilus and Cressida*:

> All the argument is a cuckold and a whore;
> A good quarrel to draw emulous factions
> And bleed to death upon.

We catch a glimpse of the busy magistrate in *Much Ado About Nothing*, when Dogberry and Verges try to tell something of urgent significance to Leonato, the most important man in town, when Leonato is busy and distracted on the morning of his only child's wedding. The patience of Magistrate Leonato with his "tedious" neighbors is understandably limited. If ambition spurred John Shakespeare to seek the office of bailiff, in private life he also entertained ideas above his station. The illiterate butcher had wooed and won Mary Arden, daughter of Robert Arden, a local country squire. The Arden house, in the village of Wilmcote, three miles north of Stratford, was far grander than the Henley Street habitation. The liberal use of timber with brick facing befit the home of an old and distinguished Warwickshire family. Robert's father was Sir Thomas Arden, who had been knighted by Henry VII. As the women of Warwickshire probably gossiped, John Shakespeare had married "up" when he took Mary Arden as his bride. Yet Mary would lose her gentry ranking when she wed a mere tradesman. Perhaps the wife's diminished status fueled her husband's aspirations. Yet John Shakespeare believed that his name had links to lines more ancient than that of the fifteenth-century Ardens.

The very name suggested the arms of a Norman knight. In French, "Shakespeare" derived from *saque-epée*, "to draw out a sword."[6] John Shakespeare must have imagined that some Norman knight with William the Conqueror had won the name for bravery in battle. Such a phrase conveyed something like what "quick on the draw" would have conveyed to a Wyatt Earp or a Matt Dillon—it would have been a motto for a knight.

For John Shakespeare to become a knight, however, he first had to become a gentleman. As a gentleman, with a coat of arms, he could then position himself for the next rank, of knighthood. John Shakespeare was determined that he would gain his coat of arms, and his son a university degree. John Shakespeare might be illiterate, but his son would be lettered. William would be sent to the royal grammar school in Stratford, which prepared boys for Oxford or Cambridge.

The local grammar school, which had been founded in the early fifteenth century, had recently been reorganized under the royal patronage of

Edward VI. In its day it was more respected than Eton, the headmaster of which only received half as much salary as the head of the King's New School of Stratford-upon-Avon.[7] The school had been blessed by a rich benefactor, Sir Hugh Clopton, a one-time lord mayor of London. Clopton was a mercer who had amassed a fortune selling silks to London's gentry; he would also erect a splendid stone bridge to replace a dilapidated wooden one. Four centuries later, travellers through town still cross the Avon River by way of Clopton Bridge.

When Will entered the school in about 1571, at age 7, he was the first son and the pride of the family. His youthful blond hair had probably not yet turned to the chestnut color it would in his manhood. A schoolboy of his time had to rise early. He would put on his clothes, tying his shirt collar to his neck, and go downstairs to salute his parents. Then he would take his satchel, books, pen, paper, and ink and head off to school, doffing his cap if addressed by any man.[8]

From the very beginning things came easily to Will Shakespeare. He was blessed by good looks and a winning personality. Merry hazel eyes would dance when he spoke, and an easy smile spread across his rosy cheeks. If he was sometimes impulsive, it was because he was so inquisitive. His retentive mind, which quickly mastered the school primers, must have endeared him to his schoolmasters.

Even so, young Will Shakespeare must not have enjoyed the school curriculum of Anglican liturgy and Latin drilling. The Latin book was *Lyly's Grammar*, and the catechism book was called the ABC. The master would face the class with book in one hand and rod in the other. Later Shakespeare's *Two Gentlemen of Verona* would "sigh like a schoolboy who had lost his ABC," and in *Love's Labour's Lost*, would be "a domineering pedant o'er the boy, than whom no mortal is so magnificent."

The bright morning countryside of Warwickshire would have tempted the young schoolboy to run instead in the elm-studded woods, perhaps with the whitish hound named Silver that Shakespeare would mention in both *The Taming of the Shrew*:

> Saw'st thou not boy, how Silver made it good
> At the hedge corner in the coldest fault?
> I would not lose the dog for twenty pound.

and *The Tempest*:

> Hey Silver! There goes Silver.

But Will's typical day was not so carefree. He had to begin his school day with 6 A.M. prayers, followed by hours of reciting conjugations and declensions of Latin verbs and nouns under the stern tutelage of Thomas Jenkins, a schoolmaster with Welsh antecedents. Years later Shakespeare would write in *The Merry Wives of Windsor* of a Welsh schoolmaster named Evans, as he quizzed a pupil named William:

Evans: Come hither, William; hold up your head: come. . . . What is "fair,"
    William?
William: Pulcher.

Evans: What is lapis, William?
William: A stone.

Woe to the pupil who did not have the right answer! For punishment, a Stratford grammar school boy was made to stand and place his hand flat upon a special desk for the schoolmaster to rap with a cane. Such a desk has been preserved and can be seen today, with numerous marks from strikings.[9] One day Shakespeare would write in *As You Like It* of

> The whining school boy, with his satchel
> And shining morning face, creeping like a snail
> Unwillingly to school.

The laws of Latin grammar were perhaps easier to master than the rules of rhetoric. "Elocutio" was part of the royal grammar school regimen. Not only did the schoolboy have to study the structure of the Latin oration, but also all of its Ciceronian rhetorical devices, which had been adapted from the Greeks. It is one thing to recognize the use of irony, allegory, or hyperbole, but the understanding and application of litotes, zeugma, and polypton would daunt a modern graduate student.[10] The Stratford lad did not forget these lessons. As a playwright he would craft scores of orations, to be mouthed by princes and the politically mighty. (In fact, the very words "orator" and "oratory" would appear in his plays no less than 45 times.)

Furthermore, the daily assignments of writing essays, as well as translating Cicero's orations and Ovid's poetry into English or Biblical passages into Latin, opened the world of words, and the almost magical properties that the right word possesses.[11]

Besides being apt, Will was a willing student, and realized what his father expected of him. Some have tried to paint Shakespeare as a rural clod, but he actually had a good education. Levi Fox, the director of the Shakespeare Birthplace Trust in Stratford from 1945 to 1984, has said that Shakespeare left the royal grammar school "with better Latin than a student who has just taken a classics degree" at today's Oxford or Cambridge.[12]

NOTES

1. A. L. Rowse and John Hedgsee, *Shakespeare's Land* (San Francisco: Chronicle Books, 1987), p. 38. Shakespeare was baptized on April 26 at the Church of the Holy Trinity. Two or three days usually passed between birth and christening, thus buttressing the Stratford belief that Shakespeare was born on St. George's Day.

2. Ibid., p. 16.

3. Joseph Quincy Adams, *A Life of William Shakespeare* (Boston: Houghton Mifflin, 1923), pp. 25–27.

4. Levi Fox, *The Shakespeare Handbook* (Boston: G. K. Hall, 1987), p. 15.

5. Peter Levi, *The Life and Times of William Shakespeare* (New York: Holt, 1988), p. 13.

6. Adams, *Life of Shakespeare*, pp. 124–26. The Great Rolls of Normandy in 1195 listed the name of William Sakeespee. From *Magni Rotoli Normaniae*, London edited by Thomas Stapleton (1840–44). N.p., n.d.

7. Adams, *Life of Shakespeare*, p. 48.

8. Francis Seager, *Schoole of Virtue* (1577), reprinted in F. J. Furnivall, *Babee's Book* (London: Early English Text Society, 1868).

9. Adams, *Life of Shakespeare*, p. 51. *The Compleat Gentleman* (London, 1622), by Henry Peachman, has these lines:

> I knew of one who in winter would ordinarily
> On a cold morning whip his boys over for
> no other reason than to get himself a heat.

10. Fox, *Shakespeare Handbook*, p. 35.

11. S. H. Burton, *Shakespeare's Life and Stage* (Edinburgh: W. & R. Chambers, 1989), p. 43.

12. Fox, *Shakespeare Handbook*, p. 32.

CHAPTER TWO

A Dream Dashed

One writ with me in sour misfortune's book!

Romeo and Juliet
act 5, scene 3

In 1575 disaster struck the Shakespeare household, and Will Shakespeare's schoolboy days came to an end. John Shakespeare was arrested by Sir Thomas Lucy, the presiding justice in Warwickshire, and fined £40. For a respected town leader such as Alderman Shakespeare, the ignominy of arrest was surely painful. But what must have shattered the illiterate glover's dreams was not the arrest, but the fine. Today £40 does not sound like so much money, yet it was just about the cost of the house in Henley Street—a double house large enough to contain his glover's store on the west side and room for his family on the east side.[1] By today's reckoning, £40 might amount to $100,000.

If John Shakespeare had not paid the fine, he would have gone to jail. What offense had Shakespeare committed to be fined such an exorbitant amount? Had he cheated on a contract, or failed to pay his taxes? No, the fine was for failure to attend church.

Today a fine or a jail sentence for such an offense seems harsh. But in Tudor times religion was the stuff of politics, and the wrong politics could spell treason.

When Henry VIII divorced Catherine of Aragon to marry Anne Boleyn, he separated England from the Church of Rome. On Henry's death, his sickly son Edward became king for six years. When Edward died, Mary Tudor, the daughter of Henry VIII and his first wife, Catherine of Aragon, returned England to the bosom of Mother Rome. History calls her Bloody Mary, for burning at the stake some English clerical leaders who refused to reconvert to Catholicism. Yet when Elizabeth succeeded Mary in 1558, she was just as ruthless in making England Protestant as her half-sister had been in enforcing Catholicism.

John Shakespeare must have been torn in his faith. He had been born both a Catholic and an Englishman. As a Catholic, he was probably uncomfortable with those new "puritans" who wanted to purify the church service from its "papist" rituals. Yet as an Englishman, he no doubt disliked the idea of an English monarch yielding to a Roman Pope who openly backed the King of Spain. At a time when nationalism was not yet a word, or high-church Anglicanism an understood concept, John could have been called an Anglo-Catholic.[2]

As an English Catholic, he as many other Englishmen, may have stopped attending his parish church when its "reforming" rector became too radical in rooting out the old rituals. John Shakespeare was not yet a gentleman, but he was a civic leader in the community and connected by marriage with the Ardens. The Ardens over the years had crossed swords in Warwickshire with the Earl of Leicester, Judge Lucy's political patron.[3] The pro-Catholic Ardens saw Leicester as an upstart who had cashed in on his intimacy with Queen Elizabeth.

As tax officials often seem to zero in on the prominent, so Justice Sir Thomas Lucy might have singled out John Shakespeare for punishment. Like the American country justice of the peace who once paid himself from fines collected by a speed trap, Sir Lucy would amass a rich estate from fines he collected by checking up on church attendance. For Lucy to fine John Shakespeare was a double bonanza; he both increased his fortune and cemented his alliance with Leicester.

For Lucy, changing religion was no more difficult than changing doublets. He had become a Catholic for Queen Mary and then a Protestant again for Queen Elizabeth. Lucy was Leicester's henchman in Warwickshire, and Leicester was Elizabeth's chief suitor and lover in England. Lucy was as opportunistic as Leicester was. Religion was a matter of convenience, not conscience. Whether his conversion improved him spiritually we do not know, but it did improve him financially.[4]

Of course, John Shakespeare paid the heavy fine, but to do so he had to mortgage most of his wife's inheritance, which included a house and land in Wilmcote and a share of two houses and land in Snitterfield. That was the land in the country that he needed to gird his claim to squiredom.

In *The Merchant of Venice* Shakespeare put Shylock in the same predicament when he was stripped of his wealth.

> You take my house, when you take the prop
> That doth sustain my house; you take my life,
> When you do take the means whereby I live.

When a family faces bankruptcy, education is a luxury. The 12-year-old had to be taken out of school and put to work. Any hope of an Oxford education had been dashed, as surely as had been his father's hope of a gentleman's coat of arms.

Will left school to work as a butcher boy.[5] Slaughtering was not the most refined of trades, but it could provide ready employment for an unskilled and unapprenticed young man. John Aubrey, born about a decade after Shakespeare died but one of the earliest to write about Shakespeare, related that "when this young Shakespeare killed a calf, he would do it in high style and make a speech."[6] In *Henry VI*–Part II, Shakespeare may have alluded to his butchering experience when the King says:

> And as the butcher takes away the calf,
> And binds the wretch and beats it when it strays,
> Beating it to the bloody slaughter house,
> Even so remorseless have they borne him hence;
> And as his dam runs lowing up and down,
> Looking the way her harmless young one went,
> And can do naught but wail her darling's loss.

We hesitate to imagine how his mother, a genteel woman and granddaughter of a knight, reacted to her favorite child being obliged to work at a butchery. Mary Arden, whose aristocratic name was associated with that of the royal woods of Warwickshire that bordered the town of Stratford, had suddenly seen her secure world come tumbling down. Yet she could not have completely blamed her husband, because John Shakespeare may have been targeted as kin to the Ardens, through her. Mary Shakespeare's pro-Catholic uncles and grandfather had resisted Leicester when the earl used his close relationship with the protestant Elizabeth against those whose loyalty to himself, as well to the new Queen, was in question.

Her son Will was now the oldest; the two daughters that preceeded him had died. Other children had followed Will—Gilbert, Joan, Anna, Richard, and Edmond. But Will, the first son, was her favorite. He might have one day become Sir William, if her husband's dreams of knighthood had not been dashed. As for Will himself, he could adjust easily. His writings showed he had disliked the discipline of school. At least, working in the butcher's shop plunged him into a man's world.

There was not a sullen bone in Will Shakespeare's body. Not one ill remark or strike in anger is recorded, even by hearsay, in all his days. Will would smile his way through life. He could find pleasure in the meanest of tasks and humor in the worst of troubles. Aubrey handed down this comment: "Will was a good honest fellow, but he darest crackt [sic] a jest with him at any time."[7] As he ripened into a young man, such winning ways made Will very attractive to the opposite sex.

As Shakespeare carved up meat in the butcherhouse, visions of prettier flesh must have danced in his mind. Young girls must have tried to catch his eye as he sold meat to their parents, or as he sang from the family pew in Holy Trinity Church. Evidently two of them—two different Annes—made marriage plans with the handsome butcher apprentice. On November 27, 1582, the records read that banns were formally announced in church for William Shakespeare's intention to marry Ann Whatley.[8] A license was issued for the marriage of "William Shaxpere and Ann Whatley of Temple Grafton." We know little of Ann Whatley, because Will did not marry her. (Some scholars believe "Whatley" was a clerical misspelling.) Instead, without any banns, on November 28, 1582, a hurry-up wedding to Anne Hathaway was arranged, by a special license from the Bishop of Worcester. Anne Hathaway was three months pregnant with Shakespeare's child.

The Hathaways were a respected Puritan family in the country, and they may have found Anne's conduct less than puritanical. The father, John Hathaway, a well-to-do farmer, had recently died, and Anne's brothers must have pressed for a marriage. Their feelings about their sister's marriage were probably more of relief than of resentment against Will, however, because at 26 the oldest Hathaway daughter was, by Elizabethan standards, an old maid. Some unkind commentators have suggested that she might have trapped Will, who was eight years her junior. In *Twelfth Night*, Shakespeare himself alludes to the difficulties of a woman, the Countess Olivia, in marrying a man much younger than herself.

Peter Levi writes in his biography, "Shakespeare seems to have been a wild and innocent young man." The Hathaway house in the little village of Shottery was but a short two-and-half-mile walk from Stratford. The garden of the house, as Levi says, gives way "to open wheatfields and must be enchanting at moonlight."[9]

We can understand why Anne Hathaway was attracted to the young Shakespeare, but what did Shakespeare see in her, other than a willing body? For one thing, a young man with the intellect of Shakespeare's may well find an older woman more stimulating and interesting than a girl his own age or younger.

In June 1583, six months after their wedding, their first child arrived. The daughter was given the Puritan name of Susanna, from the Apocrypha. In the biblical tale Susanna was known for her chastity, which might have been an ironic comment on the mother's premarriage pregnancy.

The family at first moved to the Shakespeares' crowded little house on Henley Street. But as a husband and a father, the 19-year-old Will Shakespeare would have looked for a position more suitable to a husband and head of a family. An apprenticeship in a butcher house, while it would eventually lead to a secure trade, brought little or no income. Yet his years in the grammar school might qualify him for a teaching position.

So he probably became a Stratford schoolteacher, or a tutor in a family. Although no school records exist that can document his few years of teaching, Ben Jonson would later say of him, "He had but little Latin and less Greek but he understood Latin pretty well for he had been in his younger years a school teacher."[10] Such a tutoring job or school position would have been a dead-end job, however. Shakespeare never could have risen to a headmastership, since he did not have a university degree.

If drilling young boys in Latin was financially and socially a big step up from the butchery, it was no less boring. At a time when some young Englishmen were discovering new continents, the strictures of school life must have been stifling for Shakespeare. The 1580s would be the English Renaissance—an age of adventure as well as advancement.

NOTES

1. Clara Longworth de Chambrun, *Shakespeare: A Portrait Restored* (London: Holis & Carter, 1957), p. 34.

2. Peter Levi, *The Life and Times of William Shakespeare* (New York: Holt, 1988), p. 17.

3. Ibid., p. 19.

4. Chambrun, *Shakespeare: Portrait*, p. 11.

5. Joseph Quincy Adams, *A Life of William Shakespeare* (Boston: Houghton Mifflin, 1923), pp. 62–65. Nicholas Rowe, in the first biography of Shakespeare, *Some Account of the Life etc. of Mr. William Shakespeare* (1709), wrote of Shakespeare's apprentice to a butcher. Adams thinks that Shakespeare was apprenticed to William Tyler, a butcher in Sheep Street. Shakespeare in his will did leave a ring to Tyler's son, who may have apprenticed with him. *The Traditionary Anecdotes of Shakespeare* (1838) also reported that an old town resident told a visitor in 1693 that Shakespeare had been "bound apprentice to a butcher."

6. John Aubrey, *Brief Lives Chiefly of My Contemporaries* (Oxford: J. Johnson, 1927). Some scholars question the authenticity of Aubrey, who liked to collect anecdotes about the famous, but Aubrey, who was born in 1626, interviewed theatrical people like the playhouse manager, Christopher Beeston, whose father, William Beeston, had been one of Shakespeare's acting colleagues.

7. Adams, *Life of Shakespeare*, pp. 33–34.

8. Peter Quennell, *Shakespeare: The Poet and His Background* (Cleveland: World, 1963), p. 26. Quennell suggests that the Whatley banns could have been a clerical error, as does Levi, *Life and Times of Shakespeare*. Adams, *Life of Shakespeare*, pp. 74–77, quotes from the original: "November 27, 1582, *Item eodem die similio emanavit licencia inter Wm. Shaxpere et Annam Whatley de Temple Grafton.*"

9. Levi, *Life of Shakespeare*, p. 37.

10. Quoted in Rowe, *Some Account of the Life of Shakespeare*. Nicholas Rowe was poet laureate of England. When he began searching for material on the artist he respected the most, the memory of the actor poet was still vivid in Stratford, as in London.

CHAPTER THREE

The Carpenter and Christopher

The play's the thing

Hamlet
act 2, scene 2

Will Shakespeare was a restless young man in a restless age. The bleakness of medieval times had been brightened by the Renaissance, and the discovery of the Western continents offered new horizons and vistas. New trade routes to the Orient imported not only new spices but new life-styles. As the light of morning moves westward from the east, so the creative sunshine was first seen in Italy, then spread to France, and now wended its way further westward, to England.

In our own lifetime we have seen the computer bring libraries into our living rooms. The machine marvel of the Renaissance was the printing press. The prose and poetry of Italian and French writers opened up a new world of ideas. Enlightenment was spurred by entrepreneurship—books were business. And the London printing presses clanked overtime to publish English translations of French and Italian poets and philosophers.

In the Age of Chaucer, a book was a rich man's toy; but in the Age of Shakespeare, it was becoming a staple for a growing middle class. Yet the change that was sweeping London was for the most part bypassing small towns and villages like Stratford.

In earlier medieval days a talented and creative young man might have escaped his feudal station by singing songs for knights. Such a troubador would have been the forerunner of today's rock singer. By Shakespeare's day the bard of yore had become a poet, composing not songs but sonnets, for barons and earls. With the press, the poet could now immortalize his patron with verse that all could read. Like a portrait, published poetry could be a legacy for a noble's heirs.

Sonnets, like the doublets fashionable Elizabethan men now wore, had come over from Italy. Rich young gentlemen in the court of Henry VIII had gone to Florence and Venice, in the same way old-line families in America sent their children abroad in the early part of this century. The courtiers brought back the latest styles in clothes, and in literature as well. Every Italian gentleman was supposed to be skilled at composing a 14-line poem that broke down into an octet followed by a sextet. The Elizabethans adapted the Italian sonnet into an English version, which featured twelve lines of iambic pentameter verse and closed with a rhyming couplet.

By the time of Queen Elizabeth, sonnets had become a rage in England, somewhat as crossword puzzles swept America in the 1920s. Anyone who pretended to be a gentleman proved it to his lady friend by writing a sonnet for her.

So while Will Shakespeare taught Latin verbs by day, he probably practiced writing English verse at night.[1] If he wished someday to write the masques that comprised the theatrical fare of the time, he had to polish his versifying skills.

Shakespeare's love of theater may have been first sparked when his father, while high bailiff, took him in July 1575 to Kenilworth Castle to get a glimpse of Queen Elizabeth, who was visiting the Earl of Leicester in his Warwickshire castle.[2] A probable lover of the Queen, the earl had long pressed for her hand in marriage—a marriage that would make him the most powerful lord in England. As part of his campaign to persuade the Queen to say yes, the earl had entertained her in his castle.

The Earl of Leicester knew that the Queen loved to watch theatrical entertainments, which her Puritan advisers in London frowned upon. So to honor the royal visit, the earl staged various entertainments at his Kenilworth Castle. The earl was also a theater buff, and he employed actors as his household servants so that he could stage his own entertainments. On feast days the earl would present musicals for the local Warwickshire community.

Although Will had been taken to see the Queen, it was the performance on stage that most likely captured his fancy. On that warm Monday evening the masque included a dolphin and a mermaid, and might be recalled in the lovely lines in *Midsummer Night's Dream* in which Oberon describes a mermaid singing on a dolphin's back.

> Once I sat upon a promontory
> And heard a mermaid, on a dolphin's back,
> Uttering such dulcet and harmonious breath,
> That the rude sea grew civil at her song,
> And certain stars shot madly from their spheres,
> To hear the sea-maid's music.[3]

America has many nineteenth-century stories of young men who ran off to join the circus, and twentieth-century stories of young women who chased their dreams to Hollywood. For Shakespeare the theater promised all the romance of the circus and the cinema combined.

Yet how could he, as a husband and head of a family, pull up stakes and run off to London? In 1584, at the age of 20, Shakespeare was the father of three. Following Susanna, twins had been born, a boy and a girl, named after their godparents, Hamnet and Judith Sadler, who ran a bake shop next door to the Shakespeare house.

Shakespeare must have known that if he quit his school position, his wife Anne would never go with him to London to help him seek a theatrical career. Anne was a Puritan and to Puritans the theater was Sodom and actors were sinners.[4]

The teaching position, his marriage, and the small town of Stratford all closed in on Shakespeare. What may have triggered his decision to leave Stratford was an incident at Charlecote, Sir Thomas Lucy's private park near Stratford. The best shooting was found in such private preserves. Arden Forest, which edged the town of Stratford, was Crown land, and the game that romped there—hare, woodcock, and deer—belonged to the Crown.

Shakespeare loved to hunt. In *Venus and Adonis* he writes of chasing a hare.

> Then shalt thou see the dew-bedabbled wretch
> Turn and return, indenting with the way;
> Each envious briar his weary legs do scratch,
> Each shadow makes him stop, each murmur stay.

In the centuries before cricket and golf were invented, the sport of most Englishmen was shooting game. Perhaps the free-spirited young Shakespeare had convinced himself that poaching on the preserve was no great crime—particularly if he did not get caught. Hunting may have been one of his few escapes from the confines of classroom and home.[5] Justice Lucy, who, according to legend arrested Will, may have inspired the playwright's portrait of Justice Shallow, who arrests Sir John Falstaff in *Merry Wives of Windsor*, "You . . . have killed my deer."

Shakespeare's earliest biographer, Nicholas Rowe, echoes the local tradition that the "poacher-poet" was caught by that same Justice Lucy who in 1586 had arrested Shakespeare's father. No records of a trial exist, and some presume that Shakespeare skipped the hearing and fled to London.[6]

The road through Oxford to High Wycombe and then to London was not without risk; no doubt Shakespeare carried a sword to defend himself against highwaymen. No man except a priest in cassock would have travelled without at least a dagger.[7]

When he arrived in London, the first person Shakespeare sought out was James Burbage. In 1576 Burbage, also from Warwickshire, had revolutionized the English entertainment world, by designing, building, and operating the first public theater in London, and indeed in all of Europe.[8] In fact, its name was simply the Theatre, a word Burbage himself had coined from the Greek and Latin *theatrum*. "Theatre" would become the generic name for any kind of building specifically erected for the purpose of staging plays.

Burbage had been a carpenter in the employ of the Earl of Leicester.[9] At that time, most dramatic productions were staged in the castles of noblemen, of whom Leicester was a prominent example. Villagers tended to look kindly on a local lord who would liven up their lives with a feast-day performance enacting a biblical parable, an Aesopian fable, or a kind of musical skit.

Besides helping build the stage sets, Burbage had probably taken an acting part when the Earl of Leicester entertained the Queen a decade before. Eventually Burbage decided he could make money doing what he enjoyed most—staging plays—and left Leicester's employ for London.

In the years before Burbage, dramatic performances in London were held in the law inns. The reason was that the London City Council, which was dominated by the Puritans, banned any kind of theatrical production. The City Council, however, could not police or regulate the law inns. This equivalent of our law schools answered only to the courts, whose judges and other officials were appointed by the Queen.

The audiences at the law inns, such as Gray's Inn or Middle Temple, were mostly law students, lawyers, and their merchant clients. It was the elite middle class, not the masses, who filled the hall at Gray's Inn.

Because of that, Burbage recognized an untapped market. If the villagers of Stratford loved the theatrical entertainment, would not the average Londoner? His friends discouraged him, saying that stage performances could never compete with the cockfights, boxing matches, and most popular, the bearbaiting contests, in which a bear tied to a stake would try to fight off a pack of mastiff dogs.

But where would he find a place to build his theater? If he constructed one in London proper, he would run afoul of the city authorities, who banned the stage as lewd, and sinful conduct that invited a just God's wrath. The London Council even printed posters near the law inns at the time of scheduled performances. Some of the placards read, "Players make plagues." Preachers, Puritans, and city fathers would write petitions; one preacher implored, "Will not a filthy play with a blast of trumpet, sooner call thither a thousand than a hour's telling of a bell bring to the sermon a hundred?" Most of the time the law inns ignored the politicians—except when the plague broke out. In a day when the cause of pestilent diseases was believed to be God, not germs, the plague was not only a warning but a judgment.

If Burbage wanted to stage plays in London in places other than the law inns, he had to find a way to outflank the city fathers. With money lent to him by his brother-in-law, a grocer, Burbage built his new theater on a liberty. *Liberty* was the legal term for those lands appropriated by Henry VIII from monks when he divorced the English church from Rome. The liberties, whose properties had escheated to the Crown, did not answer to the borough authorities. No ordinance by the London Council could regulate behavior or conduct that took place in a liberty.

The liberty where Burbage built his new theater was outside of the London center city and about four miles north of London Bridge off the Shoreditch Road, just east of the Finsbury Fields. It was near two amphitheaters on Southwark where the public flocked to see bearbaiting and bullbaiting. Friends told Burbage that his theatrical venture would fail, because too few would travel so far to see an afternoon performance.

True, the lords and merchants could ride out on their horses, but Burbage had built his theater not just for the rich but also for the poor. Anybody who could manage to scrape up four farthings for the afternoon's entertainment could watch as standee. For the average working man, who earned about seven shillings a week, a penny admission was about the same as a $5 movie ticket for someone who earns about $30,000 a year. In fact, Burbage bet that the big profits would lie in the pennies the masses would pay. But would the working folk who relished prize fights pay for poetry? They did, and Burbage's gamble paid off.

However, Burbage's Theatre did not ignore the richer clientele. In front of the stage he built boxes with thatched roofs for those who could pay the higher fees. He erected roofed balconies or "galleries" at an upper level around the perimeter of the hall, where barristers and prosperous merchants could sit. Behind the boxes for the lords, and below the galleries for rich middle-class patrons, was the roofless "penny pit," where the masses could stand and watch.

The "penny public" might include a yeoman from the country, a sailor off a boat, or perhaps a butcher boy, as Shakespeare had once been. Through this boisterous crowd a young damsel would sell oranges, which the audience enjoyed the way today's moviegoers devour popcorn. Not so appreciated was the lurking pickpocket, who paid his penny to snatch purses of the milling standees.

Behind the stage Burbage even installed dressing booths for the actors. This was also a theatrical first. In the castles and the law inns, actors had to scramble anywhere they could to find dressing space just off the stage.

The circular structure of the new theater added a dimension that playgoers at the inns never enjoyed. In the rounded theater they could not only see better but hear better. The roughly circular shape enhanced the visibility as well as the acoustics. The playhouse structure was wood on a brick foundation, with the exterior made of plaster ornamented with boards in the familiar Tudor style.

When Will Shakespeare came to London in 1586, it was not only the hope of acting in London's first theater that excited him but perhaps also the chance to act in one of Christopher Marlowe's new dramas, which had electrified London.

Marlowe, a classics scholar and Cambridge graduate, emulated the Greek tragedians. Like the Athenan dramatists, Marlowe put his tragic plays into poetry. Marlowe was not the first English playwright; about the first was Thomas Kyd, who wrote an earlier version of *Hamlet*. Yet Marlowe was different. He added something new: verse and the epic villain.

What thrilled Londoners was Marlowe's introduction of the diabolical figure, who would dominate the stage. His specialty was the fiendish villain, like Tamburlaine, the Tartar barbarian who butchers his way across Europe from Asia. Another monster was Barrabas in *The Jew of Malta*. In the end Barrabas and the other ogres get their just deserts. Barrabas, for example, is tossed into a boiling cauldron, to the delight of the penny standees.

Marlowe knew not only the classics but the craft of stage production. He was a born theater man, who understood the secrets of making an audience shudder. In a popular scene in *Tamburlaine*, one of the Tartar's captives was carried about in a cage and then had his back used as his conqueror's footstool. In another, the governor of Babylon was hung in chains on a wall and served as a human dart board for his taunters. Even more celebrated was the scene in which Tamburlaine made his entrance in a chariot drawn by two captive kings, with bits in their mouths like horses.

It was such a grisly spectacle that Burbage believed would attract the penny public to his new theater.[10] It could have been said about Burbage, as was once said about the actor Alfred Lunt, that "he had his head in the sky and feet in the box office." Burbage believed that an exciting story line would be something new in entertainment. Why would the working Londoners pay to see a boar attacked by a pack of mastiffs, or bare-knuckled boxers bloodying each other in a ring, if they could see a screaming Barrabas in a boiling vat?

Curiously, the ex-carpenter's vision of mass entertainment, together with a classics student's dream to write a new kind of tragedy, combined to revolutionize the stage in London.

NOTES

1. Peter Levi, *The Life and Times of William Shakespeare* (New York: Holt, 1988), p. 39.

2. Peter Quennell, *Shakespeare: The Poet and His Background* (Cleveland: World, 1963), p. 23; S. Shoenbaum, *William Shakespeare* (New York: Oxford University Press, 1987), p. 115.

3. Marquette Shute, *Shakespeare of London* (New York: Dutton, 1949), p. 21.

4. Ibid., p. 53.

5. Joseph Quincy Adams, *A Life of William Shakespeare* (Boston: Houghton Mifflin, 1923), p. 80.

6. Nicholas Rowe, *Some Account of the Life etc. of Mr. William Shakespeare* (1709).

7. *Shakespeare: Life and Work* by F. J. Furnivall and John Munro (London: Cassel, 1908).

8. Shute, *Shakespeare of London*, pp. 25–30; Adams, *Life of Shakespeare*, p. 113.

9. Shute, *Shakespeare of London*, pp. 25–30.

10. Ibid., p. 75; Adams, *Life of Shakespeare*, pp. 620–21.

CHAPTER FOUR

Apprentice Actor

To show our simple skill,
That is the true beginning of our end.

A Midsummer Night's Dream
act 5, scene 1

For a young man from Warwickshire interested in pursuing a career on the stage, Burbage's Theatre was the only place to go. When Will Shakespeare knocked on Burbage's door, Burbage's answer might have been something like this: "Will, you can start out as a prompter, but not as a player."[1]

Shakespeare would take this humble role as a beginning, just as his father had begun his municipal career in Stratford as an ale taster. In effect, Shakespeare would begin as a gofer, just as today's college student might serve as an intern in a television studio. Shakespeare did not have to go out to get coffee for the performers, but he might have had to fetch water and oats for the patrons' horses,[2] serving in a sense, as a parking attendant. Burbage, who operated a stable next to his theater, made the new apprentices do double duty in this way, and that is what Samuel Johnson tells us of the young would-be thespian's duties, in his embroidered tale of Shakespeare's apprentice days.

Shakespeare's godson, Sir William D'Avenant (see Chapter 16), would also relate that Shakespeare first won the attention of titled and moneyed theater patrons by his witty comments as he brought their horses to them after the plays.

So Will Shakespeare would be an apprentice all over again. At age 22 he would have been old compared to the other prompters. Young men in their teens, if they had any talent, soon graduated to "actresses" playing the woman's roles. But Will Shakespeare, who looked older than his years, probably could not have auditioned for a feminine part. Although he was slender, the early thinning of his auburn hair would have emphasized his large, domed forehead. Even though he had a lean frame, Shakespeare probably realized he could never make it in female roles. So he grew a mustache and a trim goatee that might age him for bit parts, as one in a crowd scene, and hoped for bigger roles later.

If he were a prompter, Shakespeare had to know not only all the roles, but the idiosyncracies of each performer playing the roles. In *Midsummer Night's Dream* he alludes to his beginnings as a prompter when he has Quince say, "Pyramus, enter: your cue is past."

Centuries later Charles Dickens would make his hero Nicholas Nickleby start as an apprentice actor when he joins Vincent Crummle's acting company. In the novel Nickleby gets on in an astonishing fashion. So did Shakespeare.

As any would-be actor, Will would have been anxious to graduate from prompter to performer. To do that, he needed a lot more than the ability to memorize a script quickly. In Elizabethan days an actor had to be an athlete. He had to leap like an acrobat, juggle like a circus performer, and fence like a knight. A young apprentice actor like Shakespeare had to practice long and hard to master the swordsmanship of the day, with rapier in the one hand while parrying with a dagger in the other. He had to learn how to duel realistically, yet without inflicting injury. For the effect of blood in savage scenes, sheep's blood was bought from a butcher. It was carried in a white leather jerkin painted to look like skin. The about-to-be-wounded actor had to arch himself just at the right moment so that the bladder could be pricked to spurt out the blood.[3]

In addition, the Elizabethan player had to train his voice. He needed not only the volume to project to the galleries but also the stamina to recite five or six lines without drawing a breath.[4] To memorize a role was no easy task. Just learning a role in one script is hard enough, but in the repertory system that was used, no two plays were given two afternoons in a row. That meant that an actor played a different character each day, and so had no time to let a role become routine.

Unlike Thomas Kyd, Robert Greene, or Christopher Marlowe, Shakespeare had experience as a player, which would make him a better playwright. In mastering his craft, Shakespeare was learning not only what made a player good but what made a play successful.[5]

The pence he pocketed as a prompter each day may not have been enough to support the wife and three children he left behind in Stratford. Some scholars refer to Stratford stories that he collected extra earnings by working as a law clerk. He would not have been the first fledgling actor to do so.[6] If this is true, what would have gained him a clerkship was his ability to read the Latin in the legal writs and deeds.

The law inns, for whom Shakespeare would later stage his first dramatic effort, were hotbeds of theatrical fans and supporters, in a city with an official policy condemning actors. Although no direct proof of legal clerkship exists, intricate knowledge of the law is apparent in the plays Shakespeare would later write. Admiralty in *Merchant of Venice*, criminal law in *Measure for Measure*, treason in *Henry V*, trespass in *Merry Wives of Windsor*, and real property in his sonnets—all could be cited as examples of Shakespeare's knowledge of the law.

As a law clerk Shakespeare would have been a witness to hundreds of real-life dramas: a neighbor's quarrel over property lines, a shopkeeper's dispute over a forged contract, or even a lover's breach of promise suit. Such scenes Shakespeare might have stored away for future dramatic use.

Whatever Shakespeare observed, he would add to what he had already read about. In a day when the printed page was still as new and as exciting a revolution in our learning life as the computer is for the young today, Shakespeare was an omnivorous reader. He read every tract or book he could lay his hands on.

Like other Elizabethan dramatists, Shakespeare would scan any novella from the Continent for ideas for new plays.[7] What he read he retained, and he could recite from memory whole passages that he had earlier perused. Some of the lines he most remembered were from his youth, such as Latin lines with the rich imagery of Ovid, and English lines from scripture in the Geneva translation of the Bible—particularly the parables from Matthew and Luke, as well as the Psalms and Proverbs.

London in 1586 was teeming with excitement, energy, and an air of destiny. Although it was only 90 miles southeast of Stratford, it might have been on another planet. A country town like Stratford, with a mere 2,000 population, could not compare with a city of 200,000 that throbbed with merchants expanding the woolen trade, shippers opening new trade routes to Asia, and publishers speeding up the printing presses to meet the growing demand for books. London was at that time the biggest European city north of Rome.[8]

Queen Elizabeth's London was Renaissance in spirit but in structure it was still medieval. It was still surrounded by a defensive wall, guarded by the Tower, and crowned by the old Cathedral of St. Paul. London in 1586 was a city of narrow streets, open sewers, wooden houses without sanitation or an adequate water supply. As a result, fire and the plague were constant threats.

Shakespeare himself found lodgings in Shoreditch (North London) not far from the Theatre. If his wife Anne ever considered joining her husband in London, surely his Puritan in-laws would have protested against any visit she and her children might make to this particular neighborhood, which was a sixteenth-century version of a red-light district.[9] Shakespeare lived in a sleazy section where brothels competed with bearbaiting arenas, boxing rings, and cockpits for the Londoner's amusement shilling.

Yet Shakespeare had come at a fortunate time. He arrived when London theater was just coming into its own, and translations from Italy and France had begun to inspire England's own Renaissance. The root of Shakespeare's artistry was his own, but it was London that supplied the atmosphere for it to flourish.

NOTES

1. Joseph Quincy Adams, *A Life of William Shakespeare* (Boston: Houghton Mifflin, 1923), pp. 126–28.

2. Ibid.

3. Marquette Shute, *Shakespeare of London* (New York: Dutton, 1949), pp. 86–90.

4. Ibid.

5. Ibid., p. 93.

6. Peter Quennell, *Shakespeare: The Poet and His Background* (Cleveland: World, 1963), p. 25.

7. Adams, *Life of Shakespeare*, p. 56.

8. William Neilson and Ashley Thorndike, *The Facts about Shakespeare* (New York: Macmillan, 1921), p. 65; *Shute, Shakespeare of London*, pp. 58–70.

9. Shute, *Shakespeare of London*, pp. 53–57.

CHAPTER FIVE

Night of Errors

My salad days
When I was green in judgement

Antony and Cleopatra
act 5, scene 1

In his early twenties, as he apprenticed on stage, Shakespeare was barely eking out a living, and no doubt he thought of ways he could employ profitably his skill with the pen. Having tried his hand at poetry, he now turned to plays.[1] *The Comedy of Errors*, a play that he might have begun as an assistant schoolteacher in Stratford, he now repolished.[2]

Shakespeare had turned to the playwright Plautus to imitate. The Roman dramatist, in *Menaechmi*, had used twins as a comic device, but Shakespeare added a second pair of twins, doubling the confusion. The adventures of the two pairs of young men take them wandering around Ephesus (a seaport of the Mediterranean), unaware of each other's existence. They are relentlessly and comically mistaken for one another in a crescendo of confusions, until the climax, when the two pairs of brothers sort out their identities.

The play takes place in one day in a single location and is thus a rare example of Shakespeare observing the classical unities of time and place. Only established artists can expect to be permitted to flout the rules.

In the artificial style that was then in vogue, Shakespeare wrote this comedy in the fashion of an Italian farce. If the shortest of all his plays had more puns than plot, it was good comedy. One laugh was a complicated wordplay on "hour" and "whore," which in Elizabethan London were pronounced the same way.

The conversation clatters in belabored rhymes, in the style of the first comic plays that competed with the masques and musical skits. Rhymes were nonmusical lyrics, which jingled in the listeners' heads long after they left the performance. Though Shakespeare's rhymes, following the accepted convention of a comedy, may have rattled like dry bones, the failure was not all Shakespeare's. He had particularly tailored his drama to please the students who resided at the law inns. After all, when he began writing, the law inns were where most plays were staged. His first theatrical attempt was called *The Comedy of Errors*,[3] but those who saw it performed called it "The Night of Errors."[4] Shakespeare's first was a flop!

The real entertainment of the evening turned out to be, not Shakespeare's play, but some unrehearsed revelry by the students. During Christmas break, the Gray's Inn students were entertaining fellow students from the Middle Temple. It would have been something like Harvard students hosting visitors from Yale, if it were some hundreds of years ago when the first crude versions of the Hasty Pudding Show appeared. The bawdy parodies and ribald songs of the Gray's Inn students and their women friends prompted retaliation by the Middle Temple students. The revue eventually turned into a riot; too much ale had made the skits go on too long. By the time Shakespeare's play was presented it was past midnight.[5] The labored repartee in this play about two Italian twins and their switched lives and loves can even translate well in the twentieth century. Yet, the polished turn of phrase in the play was lost on the drunken students.

For Shakespeare, the barge ride back down the Thames with his fellow players late that night must have been a long one. He must have been drained by the ordeal and disappointed by the outcome. Yet Shakespeare had the ability to laugh at himself as well as others.

Shakespeare's first biographer, John Aubrey, quotes a fellow actor's comments about the young man's charming manners in the late 1580s. "He was a handsome, well-shaped man, very good company, and of a very ready and pleasant smooth wit." Aubrey also wrote that they thought "he acted exceeding well" and that "he understood Latin pretty well for he had been a schoolmaster in the country."[6]

If the premiere of Shakespeare's first play ended less than happily, Shakespeare nevertheless had proved his writing skill to the Burbage company, and the Theatre would later include *Comedy of Errors* in its repertoire of scripts. As he matured, he would rely less on rhyme and more on the richness of figurative expression. The growing, if modest, popularity of the play, was however Shakespeare's first solid step in becoming a playwright. Even in this first attempt, the magic of the world's most enduring dramatist is glimpsed. Four centuries later the popular musical *The Boys from Syracuse* would be an adaptation of *The Comedy of Errors*.

NOTES

1. Peter Levi, *The Life and Times of William Shakespeare* (New York: Holt, 1988), p. 39; Joseph Quincy Adams, *A Life of William Shakespeare* (Boston: Houghton Mifflin, 1923), p. 133.

2. Tucker Brooke, *Shakespeare of Stratford* (New Haven, Conn.: Yale University Press, 1926), p. 121.

3. Brooke, *Shakespare of Stratford*, p. 121.

4. Adams, *Life of Shakespeare*, pp. 210–12; E. K. Chambers, *William Shakespeare* (Oxford: Clarendon Press, 1930), pp. 320–27.

5. Adams, *Life of Shakespeare*, pp. 211–14.

6. John Aubrey, *Brief Lives Chiefly of My Contemporaries* (Oxford: J. Johnson, 1927), p. 31.

CHAPTER SIX

Chronicles and Kings

Thereby hangs a tale

As You Like It
act 2, scene 7

If he was a former schoolmaster, Shakespeare would have brought with him to his Shoreditch lodgings at least three books. One would have been the Geneva translation of the Bible; another a new translation of *Plutarch's Lives*; and the third a 3,000-page tome, Raphael Holinshed's *Chronicles of England, Scotland, and Ireland*.[1] Holinshed had written the first history of Britain that was printed in English, not Latin. He had written up tales from as far back as the days of Briton chieftains to as recently as the era of recent Tudor monarchs. Having no wish to offend the reigning royal family, Holinshead represented the House of Tudor as the culmination of the destiny of the English, from their shrouded beginnings as Celtic island warriors to Shakespeare's day.

Just as the twentieth-century historian Arthur Schlesinger would disparage Republican presidents and exalt the names of Franklin Roosevelt and John Kennedy, Holinshed blackened the reputation of the Plantagenet Richard III and glorified the reign of the Tudor Henry VIII.

Yet the biggest event ever in English history was not to be read about in Holinshed's *Chronicles*. It was to take place in 1588, while Shakespeare first lived in London. This event was the destruction of the Spanish Armada. Sir Francis Drake slew the Spanish leviathan, much as Saint

George was supposed to have killed the dragon. To be in London that year must have been like being in Philadelphia in 1776 or London in 1945: the sinking of the massive flotilla sent English patriotism soaring. The English David had triumphed over the Spanish Goliath.

Catholic Spain in the late 1580s, as would Nazi Germany in the late 1930s, loomed over Europe. Together with the lands it dominated, Spain controlled much of what is today Austria and Italy, as well as parts of Germany and France. Beyond Europe, it held sway over North Africa. When Spain seized hold of the Netherlands, the English feared it was going to be a Hapsburg launching place for invading their little island across the Channel. And then there were the Spanish discoveries of gold in the Americas, which enabled the conquistadores to bring back to Madrid enough treasure to outfit the largest fleet the world had ever seen.

Yet little England, which covered not much more than half of an island, had triumphed over mighty Spain. If the penny public had come out in droves to watch Marlowe's epic about Tamburlaine, the Tartar conqueror, they would surely pay to see England's own history on stage. It was a time when Englishmen were proving themselves in the world, and their past would be a new source of pride.

Shakespeare sensed that Elizabethan audiences, particularly those in the penny pit, yearned for something more than rewrites of Italian love tales or Greek legends. *The Famous Victories of Henry V*, which was enacted in 1586, had suggested the public taste for history. Like a writer of modern television documentary, he would stage for English audiences an enactment of their own history, based on Holinshed's *Chronicles*.

Centuries before television, movies, and magazine photographs, Shakespeare would offer something close to visual history. The first chronicle he wrote was *Henry VI*, which was presented in three parts. Only a very self-confident young man would have ventured to turn the confused mass of quarrels and counter-plots recorded by Holinshed into manageable material, and only a young man who was experienced in the practical problems of the theater could have succeeded.

Yet in sorting out the complex intrigues, Shakespeare would find that Henry VI's life and times offered an array of interesting characters: Henry, the monarch who yearned to be a monk ("whose bookish rule hath pulled fair England down"); Joan of Arc, the French maiden whom God told to be a soldier; the French Dauphin who would be king; his mother Queen Margaret, the "she-wolf" of France who ruled instead; and back in England, Warwick, the "setter up and puller down of kings" who played off Yorkist and Lancastrian claimants to the English crown as a puppeteer would pull the strings to his dolls. Edward, the Prince of Wales, would say of Warwick in *Henry VI–Part I*:

> If that be right which Warwick says is right
> There is no wrong, but everything is right.

Shakespeare was no political scientist (the phrase was not invented until the twentieth century), but he was, in a sense a political philosopher. He may have had only a little Greek, as his rival Ben Jonson later sniffed, but it must have been enough to be familiar with the political philosopher Aristotle. Surely he also read the most widely read political handbook of his day, *The Prince*, because in his plays he refers to Machiavelli on five occasions.

Shakespeare would pack into the scripts of these and his later plays some of his own political advice and adages, which would rival those of the Florentine. The Henry VI plays, for example, contain these aphorisms:

For how can tyrants safely govern home, unless they purchase great alliance?

Soft courage makes your followers faint.

Delays have dangerous ends.

whose large style agrees not with the leanness of his purse

small things that make base men proud

What is pomp, rule, reign, but earth and dust?

Civil dissension is a viperous worm that gnaws the bowels of the commonwealth.

The presence of a king engenders love amongst his subjects.

Thrice is he armed that hath his quarrel just.

In his famed oration on opportunism, Gloucester, the future Richard III, would compare himself to Machiavelli.

> I can play the orator as well as Nestor
> Deceive more slyly than Ulysses could
> And like a Sinon take another Troy;
> I can add colour, to the chameleon
> Change shapes with Proteus to advantage
> And set the murderous Machiavell to school.

Shakespeare's chronicle was about power, a pursuit of power that brimmed with passion, or more precisely hate—the hatred of Warwick for Edward IV, of the revolutionary Jack Cade for the nobility, of Queen

Margaret for the Duchess of Gloucester, of the French for the English, and of the House of York for the House of Lancaster.

If most of us today could not read or write, and if there were no electronic media, or even newspapers or magazines with pictures people could look at, then the only history we would know would be tales about George Washington crossing the Delaware or Lincoln being shot at Ford's Theater—stories that are passed down from generation to generation by word of mouth. In Shakespeare's England there were not even illustrations of famous personages or historic battles, to be seen in public art galleries.

Imagine today's theatergoer telling a friend he has just seen a play about the American Civil War. "Why, you can see Lincoln in a cabinet meeting at the White House, and Gen. Robert E. Lee meeting with his staff in a tent!" But such might have been the effect of the Henry VI plays on the penny public.[2] With the help of these plays the Elizabethans could see their country's civil war—the struggle for the Crown between the Houses of York and Lancaster—and the English invasion across the Channel to secure Plantagenet holdings in France. It is a three-play drama about courage, martial prowess, and the noble righteousness of the English, as represented by such loyal and able leaders as Salisbury, Bedford, Warwick, and above all Lord Talbot, opposite the opportunism, treachery, and sneakiness of the French represented by the depraved La Pucelle.

In *Henry VI–Part I*, English audiences thrilled to the derring-do against the French of captains like Talbot:

> Bring forth the body of old Salisbury,
> And here advance it in the market-place,
> The middle centre of this cursed town
> Now have I paid my vow unto his soul;
> For every drop of blood was drawn from him
> There hath at least five Frenchmen died to-night.

The three-play drama of Henry VI with all its action, was not unlike the early movie serials in its appeal to the unsophisticated—hand-to-hand fighting and cannon volleys, not to mention all the fanfare of funerals and other processions of state, punctuated by drum rolls and trumpet flourishes. The success of this first Henry VI play led to a sequel and then another sequel—*Henry VI–Part I*, *Henry VI–Part II*, and *Henry VI–Part III*. Hollywood did not originate the idea of exploiting a market by writing sequels to a popular production. This trilogy would be the stage history of England's War of the Roses.

When Shakespeare had exhausted the story of Henry VI, he had to look for something else that would capture the popular fancy. What other figure in English history would the penny public come out in droves to see on stage?

Today, many a paperback thriller on the newsstands has a cover adorned by a swastika or shows the face of Hitler in the background. Even after half a century, any book involving Hitler and the Nazis is a surefire lure.

So Shakespeare's answer was easy: Richard III. The nastiest villain in English history, at least according to Tudor chronicler Holinshed, was the Plantagenet Richard III. Here was an ogre worth hissing. Old Queen Margaret calls him "the slave of nature and son of Hell," "that bottled spider," and "this hunch-backed toad." Why, this hunchbacked maniac had killed his own nephews in his bloody seizure of the crown! Like the acclaimed Marlowe, Shakespeare would build his whole drama around the Holinshed-depicted monster.

The famous soliloquy

> Now is the winter of our discontent
> Made glorious summer by this sun of York

with which Richard opens the play is the best rhetoric Shakespeare had yet written, and it goes on to describe the speaker's special brand of villainy:

> Since I cannot prove a lover,
> To entertain these fair well-spoken days,
> I am determined to prove a villain,
> And hate the idle pleasures of these days.

In the 1970s when Richard Nixon was a demon to the political left, Sir Laurence Olivier in a film played Richard in a way that suggested a Nixon to some. Actually, Shakespeare had in mind the two-faced courtier and palace politician Sir Walter Raleigh when Richard confides to the audience:

> And thus I clothe my naked villainy
> With odd ends stolen out of holy writ;
> And seem a saint, when most I play the devil.[3]

Shakespeare's dark poetry brings to mind lines from Marlowe's *Faustus*. But to the academic and intellectual community in the 1970s the lamentful soliloquy of Richard III seemed to conjure up the Watergate-embattled Richard Nixon:

> My conscience hath a thousand several tongues,
> And every tongue brings in a several tale,
> And every tale condemns me for a villain.
> Perjury, perjury
>
>   . . .
>   'Guilty! guilty!'
> I shall despair, no creature loves me.

When Richard III cries out at the end, "A horse! a horse! my kingdom for a horse!" modern audiences may hear the desperation of a Nixon saying "The tapes! The tapes! I should have burned the tapes."

The Olivier of Shakespeare's time was Richard Burbage, the son of the Theatre owner. But Richard Burbage, in his charismatic appeal to audiences, was more like a Richard Burton. The resonant timbre of his voice could sound a charge, cry a lament, confide his plots, or express his love. Burbage, in other words, had presence.

Haunting eyes stared out of his face, which had a beard that enhanced his strongly chiseled chin. Burbage was the company's star performer, and he came to own the role of Richard III much as the movie actor George C. Scott would be General Patton. Burbage was so identified with Richard III that a hundred years later, when a guide was taking visitors through Bosworth Field, he said, "And there's where old Dick Burbage cried, 'A horse! a horse! my kingdom for a horse!'"[4]

In the London taverns they were soon shouting Richard III's dying cry. Shakespeare had made Burbage a household word.

Shakespeare was not above pulling a prank on his friend Dick Burbage. It is told that on one occasion a sixteenth-century "groupie" had arranged a tryst with the matinee idol directly after the play's afternoon performance. Burbage had had "King Richard III" emblazoned on his door. Just as the performance ended, Shakespeare let himself into the room before Burbage. When the anxious lady knocked on the door, whispering, "King Richard III?" Shakespeare answered, "No, this is William the Conqueror. Know ye, that before Richard III, in line of succession, came William the Conqueror".[5]

Shakespeare might have lacked the panache of Richard Burbage or Richard Burton, but he quickly mounted the ladder in the James Burbage company from apprentice to a leading performer. It is thought that he had an underplayed professionalism that lent credibility to character roles which too often had become stereotyped.

Even without the makeup or costume, Shakespeare had an aura of dignity with his slender stature and elegant grace. His mustache and goatee enhanced the nobility of his imposing head. Yet with his working class background, Shakespeare was relaxed and unpretentious.

Shakespeare took his work seriously but not himself. His early biographer, Nicholas Rowe, had the advantage of speaking to a few who remembered Shakespeare. He wrote: "Besides the advantages of his wit he was in himself a good natured man, of great sweetness in his manners and a most agreeable companion".[6] He lacked the usual egocentricity associated with actors and artists. By every account he was known for his unfailing courtesy to others and his constant good humor about himself.

Shakespeare identified with the audience that came to Burbage's Theatre. He scripted patriotic themes out of their history for them, because he was a patriot himself. Pageantry and politics would be the formula for his scripts and the recipe for his success.

NOTES

1. William Neilson and Ashley Thorndike, *The Facts about Shakespeare* (New York: Macmillan, 1921), pp. 50–66.

2. Alfred Harbage, *Shakespeare's Audience* (New York: Columbia University Press, 1941), p. 159.

3. Peter Quennell, *Shakespeare: The Poet and His Background* (Cleveland: World, 1963), pp. 107–8, 147.

4. Joseph Quincy Adams, *A Life of William Shakespeare* (Boston: Houghton Mifflin, 1923), p. 216.

5. S. Schoenbaum, *William Shakespeare* (New York: Oxford University Press, 1987), p. 205.

6. Nicholas Rowe, *Some Account of the Life etc. of Mr. William Shakespeare* (1709).

CHAPTER SEVEN

Atrocious and Andronicus

On horror's head horrors accumulate.

Othello
act 3, scene 3

By the early 1590s the actor Shakespeare was doubling as chief script writer for the Burbage company.[1] In fact, Shakespeare was the only one in London who was both a performer and a playwright.[2] Naturally, Burbage, as the head of the company, must have looked to Will to come up with another crowd pleaser, to follow the success of *Richard III*.

Today's movie and television writers comb novels for plots with action-filled scenarios in which fists fly, guns are fired, and passions clash. So Shakespeare must have sifted through old plays and plots to find one that would appeal to the standees, whose pennies for tickets to *Richard III* had made the Burbage troupe a most profitable company. Though the plot Shakespeare came up with would be his supreme box office success, it was not *Hamlet*, nor *Macbeth*, but a play rarely staged or even read today—*Titus Andronicus*.[3]

Richard III ended with the king's crown rolling in the dust of Bosworth Field. Shakespeare would top that in *Titus Andronicus*, in which it was heads that rolled. Aaron the Moor was a villain to make Richard III envious.

Titus Andronicus had already been the subject of a crude play by George Peele.[4] Shakespeare, like Peele, loosely based his plot on the Roman leader

Titus, a figure in *Plutarch's Lives*. In Shakespeare's drama, Andronicus
has one hand chopped off before the audience, and his two sons' severed
heads are brandished on stage. Lavinia, Titus's daughter, whose tongue
has been ripped out and her hands cut off, picks up her father's severed
hand with her teeth. Later Titus kills the two men who have raped Lavinia
and helps her cook up a pie. She holds a basin between the stumps of her
hands to catch the blood of the men who raped her, and her father serves
it up in a dessert for the rapists' mother to eat. This was a Marlovian drama,
but the villainy of Aaron the Moor is more terrible than that of Tamburlaine, more bestial than that of Barrabas. Aaron proclaims:

> Vengeance is in my heart, death in my hand,
> Blood and revenge are hammering in my head.

Even Stephen King, the best-selling author of horror books today, would
be hard-pressed to write a book or film script to equal such a banquet of
blood. In savagery that makes Saddam Hussein seem subdued by comparison, Aaron the Moor boasts of his badness:

> Few come within the compass of my curse—
> Wherein I did not some notorious ill:
> As kill a man, or else devise his death;
> Ravish a maid, or plot the way to do it;
> Accuse some innocent, and forswear myself;
> Set deadly enmity between two friends;
> Make poor men's cattle break their necks;
> Set fire on barns and hay-stacks in the night,
> And bid the owners quench them with their tears.
>   . . .
> Tut I have done a thousand dreadful things
> As willingly as one would kill a fly;
> And nothing grieves me heartily indeed,
> But that I cannot do ten thousand more.

It is an apt description of an unfeeling tragedy, that most theaters
through the centuries have found too gory to stage. Though Shakespeare's gruesome spectacle of torture and mutilation was ignored by
repertories for centuries, it was revived by Sir Laurence Olivier's London company just after World War II, when fresh memories of Nazi
barbarism made such atrocities all too believable. Viewers in London
would leave the theater mentally and physically sick. In Elizabethan
England, the gruesome play about the Roman leader brought record

crowds not only in London but also when it was taken to the hinterland cities such as Bath and Bristol.[5]

In an era when audiences were not the docile middle-class patrons of today's theater, the penny standees screamed their delight when Lavinia's assaulters were killed. Like a baseball game in New York's Shea Stadium, or a soccer game in England's Liverpool, the spectators cheered and booed lustily.[6]

The atrocity of Aaron offered Shakespeare a chance to inject his own political conservatism: Reaction to cruelty should not beget its own cruelty, nor should response to tyranny spawn its own tyranny.

Shakespeare has the noble Roman Marcus say to Titus:

O Brother speak to me of possibilities
And do not break off into deep extremes.

Marcus again warns Titus:

Order well the state
That like events may ne'er it ruinate.

Shakespeare had given gore to the penny public, but he had offered the blood in blank verse. He appealed to the sensitivities of both the crude and the cultured, and he delighted both. The man Ben Jonson would call "gentle" for his sunny nature could by pen depict the most grisly horrors. Jonson himself would actually kill a man, and other poets of the age, such as Sydney, Surrey, Wyatt, Raleigh, and Marlowe, did not die in their own beds. Yet not one deed of mayhem, assault, or violence stained Shakespeare's life.

Poets in the sixteenth century were more like F. Scott Fitzgerald, William Buckley, or George Plimpton—playboys, yachtsmen, and amateur athletes. They were swashbuckling aristocrats who created their own romantic world of duels and derring-do. A Renaissance gentleman prided himself on being at once poet, philosopher, scientist, athlete, and soldier.

Actors were not gentlemen. They were in the entertainment business, bracketed with fist fighters, jugglers, acrobats, and clowns. Actors were "roustabouts," only marginally above the status of prostitutes. The gulf between a cavalier poet and a professional performer was almost as wide socially as that between a professor and a professional wrestler today.

In Elizabethan days the university graduate would hone his skills in versifying as he would his footwork in fencing. Almost every rich and landed family had one son who deemed himself a poet. But if all who scripted plays had to be poets, very few poets were playwrights—but Shakespeare was both a successful actor and a writer.

Shakespeare was first an actor, and his skills as an actor made him a superb playwright. On the stark stage of Shakespeare's day, the richness lay in the poetry, not in the sets. For an actor and playwright, it was always the words that mattered most. Shakespeare wrote for a theater in which language was king. And that language was the developing English tongue, which he would enoble and exalt.

Burbage hired Shakespeare in 1586, which proved to be the wisest investment Burbage ever made. Shakespeare used his script-writing talents to make himself the most indispensable man in the Burbage company. The company raked in receipts from Shakespeare's crowd-pleasing chronicles, to become London's most profitable theatrical group.

Shakespeare was not only actor and playwright; he might have helped with props and costumes. Usually costumes were found from servants who had received cast-off garments from their lords. The stage manager, who spent the company's money, faced an array of budget decisions. Could they afford to hire another trumpeter for a royal procession? Would a new robe have to be bought for the Roman Titus Andronicus, or would Richard III's garment do?[7]

Today, books abound about Shakespeare's "tragic vision" or his insight into "love's healing power" or his sense of "human destiny," but students will gain a better understanding of Shakespeare by concentrating on him as a man of the theater.

Shakespeare was not the star actor of the company, but he was the writer. But just as a Hollywood screenwriter has little say about how his original effort will be changed or revised, so an Elizabethan playwright would surrender his scripts to the acting company. Just as today's television and movie studios have to meet an insatiable demand, so Shakespeare had to skim through old Latin dramas and Italian romances for material he could adapt to new plays.

Once Shakespeare saw possibilities in a plot, he could dash off the verse so quickly that, out of envy, some playwrights damned him for lack of scholarship. It sometimes seemed that Shakespeare could pen verse faster than others could write prose.

Jonson denounced Shakespeare's facility of writing. Shakespeare's effortless genius, and the jealousy it provoked, is reminiscent of the composer Salieri's envy of Mozart in the film *Amadeus*. Mozart tells Salieri that he composed as if God were dictating to him, but Salieri preferred to believe that it was the devil. When the poet Robert Browning was asked what he admired most about Shakespeare, he replied, "The royal ease with which he walks up the steps and takes his seat upon the throne while we poor fellows have to struggle hard to get up a step or two."[8] Shakespeare shared with Mozart not only the gift of genius but more precisely a "fabulous" aural memory. The words of any spoken line, be it a Latin verse he once recited in his school days or a passage from a play he once heard, would be indelibly etched in his mind.

One older playwright who was especially incensed by the Shakespearean spate of new plays was Robert Greene. A self-appointed literary lion in London circles, the red-bearded Greene wrote not only plays and poems, but prose romances and essays on social life. Literature was his profession, and he resented Shakespeare as an "upstart." To Greene, Shakespeare was a "roustabout" actor with no education, who was succeeding in a calling he had no right to be in. And even worse, Shakespeare was making so much money when real poets and writers who had university degrees made so little. What enraged Greene was that Shakespeare did not belong to the "club." By his attack Greene hoped to enlist the opposition of established playwrights with university credentials, such as Christopher Marlowe and George Peele.

Greene sneered at this actor who dared to be a playwright, comparing Shakespeare to the crow in Aesop's fable who decked himself out in borrowed plumage. "There is an upstart crow, beautified with our feathers with his tiger's heart wrapped in a player's hide, [he] supposes he is as well able to bombast out blank verse as the best of you and being an absolute *Johannes Factotum* [Johnny Do-All] is, in his own conceit the only Shake-scene in a country."[9] By "Shake-scene," Greene was charging that Shakespeare was a mere hack who dashed off plays in slap-dash fashion. And *Johannes Factotum* described a Shakespeare who juggled the jobs of acting, set designing, and directing, as well as play writing. The phrase "O tiger's heart wrapped in a player's hide!" was a reference to Shakespeare's dramatic success, *Henry VI–Part III*, in which Queen Margaret is described as a "tiger's heart in a woman's hide."

Burbage and Shakespeare's fellow actors may have been upset by the attack, but Shakespeare himself seemed to have shrugged it off. His temperament, rare among artists, seems to have been able to smile away the worst of smears.

Though a bard, Shakespeare was also a businessman.[10] Plays like *Titus Andronicus*, *Richard III*, and the three chronicles of *Henry VI* were as successfully received as they were speedily written. Yet the profits did not so much come to Shakespeare as a playwright, but as a performer who shared in the proceeds of the Burbage company. Since it was the only joint stock company in the period, Shakespeare prospered as the company flourished. By scripts that exploited history as well as horror, Shakespeare had earned a fame second only to that of Marlowe, and a commercial success for his acting company second to none.

NOTES

1. William Neilson and Ashley Thorndike, *Facts about Shakespeare* (New York: Macmillan, 1921), p. 92.

2. Marquette Shute, *Shakespeare of London* (New York: Dutton, 1949), p. 130.

3. Ibid., p. 98; according to Peter Quennell, *Shakespeare: The Poet and His Background* (Cleveland: World, 1963), p. 139, "*Titus Andronicus* delighted the sensation-loving 'penny-knaves.' " Joseph Quincy Adams, *A Life of William Shakespeare* (Boston: Houghton Mifflin, 1923), p. 135, quotes the introduction to Ben Jonson's *Bartholomew Fair*, 1614: "He that will swear *Jeronimo* or *Andronicus* are the best plays yet shall pass unaccepted here as a man whose judgment shows it is constant and hath stood still these five and thirty years."

4. Adams, *Life of Shakespeare*, p. 134.

5. Shute, *Shakespeare of London*, p. 195.

6. S. H. Burton, *Shakespeare's Life and Stage* (Edinburgh: W. & R. Chambers, 1989), p. 196.

7. Joseph Papp and Elizabeth Kirkland, *Shakespeare Alive* (New York: Viking, 1989), pp. 126–27.

8. Quoted in F. J. Furnivall and John Munro, *Shakespeare: Life and Work* (London: Cassel, 1908), p. 168.

9. Quoted in Adams, *Life of Shakespeare*, p. 139.

10. Quennell, *Shakespeare*, p. 64.

CHAPTER EIGHT

Lovers and Lenders

Here's much to do with hate, but more with love.

Romeo and Juliet
act 1, scene 1

Elizabethan playwrights had no copyrights. The big profits came from the selling of tickets, not scripts.[1] What the writer scripted for the acting company became the company's property, and the actors would not let a good script out of their sight, for it was money in the bank. To have a script printed in a playbook was commercial suicide, since once a playbook appeared on the stalls, anybody could buy a copy and have the play staged. So to sell a script was bad business.

Shakespeare's plays, however, had begun to develop a following. With *Titus Andronicus* he had solidified his appeal to the illiterate poor, but perhaps he now wanted to extend that appeal to the literate poor—the students. He effectively did so in 1593 with a love story, *Romeo and Juliet.*[2]

Imagine Shakespeare coming home to his lodgings at Shoreditch Road after a performance at the Theatre, and perhaps having some cakes and a pint of beer at the Mermaid Tavern. Once he was set on writing a love story, he must have turned in his mind Arthur Brooke's recently published narrative poem, "The Tragical History of Romeus and Juliet," which in turn had been adapted from an Italian novella. Shakespeare no doubt had read the Brooke work, and he must have found it tedious, or he would not have revamped the love poem in the way he did. For one thing, the Puritan in Brooke had been disapproving of the unwed couple's love.[3] And then, Brooke's 3,000 lines of sing-song rhyme is maudlin. Finally, the nine-month romance was too long for stage purposes.

So in writing his script, Shakespeare cut the action to four-and-a-half days and then chopped off a few years of Juliet's age to make the romance more daring. He had to have someone tell the audience of the two clans' feud

> Two households . . .
> From ancient grudge break to new mutiny

so he added a chorus. He then added a pinch of servant comedy and a dash or two of sword-fighting—interspersed with the most beautiful poetry ever written—and a wooden poem became a timeless tragedy.

As Marquette Shute hypothesizes in *Shakespeare of London*:

He evidently wrote in white heat, once he had the paper in front of him. . . . The original script, with its suggested cuts in the margin, seems to have been used just as it was except that the loose sheets were stitched together and enclosed in some kind of wrapper.[4]

Yet if Shakespeare wrote *Romeo and Juliet* primarily for the university crowd, he did not forget his penny public. The coarse puns about "maiden heads" by the servants in the very beginning of the play must have triggered raucous laughter from the penny standees. Mercutio, also, who believes in lust, not love, is a fount of genial obscenities.

Shakespeare also spliced in the swordplay—the equivalent of a cop or cowboy shoot-out on television. Mercutio, of one old Verona family, is provoked into challenging Tybalt, a professional swordsman of a rival family. Romeo, a Montague like his friend Mercutio, is forced by the code of the clan to fight Tybalt, a Capulet, and kills him. For the slaying, Romeo is banished.

In the meantime Juliet, a Capulet, and Romeo, a Montague, have fallen in love. Juliet is no silent sonnet mistress, a passive object of male desire, but a passionate partner. She muses about the identity of her forlorn lover—"A rose by any other name would smell as sweet." The story of the two "star-crossed" lovers of rival clans would inspire countless love stories to follow, such as the twentieth-century musical *West Side Story* or the best-selling novel *Love Story* by Erich Segal, which matched a scion of a WASP family with a young Jewish woman. *Romeo and Juliet* is a tragedy not of character, but of fate.

As already noted, *Romeo and Juliet* became the rage of Oxford and Cambridge students.[5] In a day when many marriages were arranged by parents, young men must have identified with the plight of Romeo. Every student in England knew the line "O Juliet, I will lie with thee tonight." Centuries before pinups, it is said that replicas of the Capulet coat of arms were hung in the bedroom cells in Oxford and Cambridge. One can visualize Oxford or Cambridge students mooning about, reciting the play's intimate lines.

Romeo: If I profane with my unworthiest hand
    This holy shrine, the gentle sin is this,
    My lips, two blushing pilgrims, ready stand
    To smooth that rough touch with a tender kiss.
Juliet: Good pilgrim, you do wrong your hand too much,
    Which mannerly devotion shows in this;
    For saints have hands that pilgrims' hands do touch,
    And palm to palm is holy palmers' kiss.
Romeo: Have not saints lips and holy palmers too?
Juliet: Ay, pilgrim, lips that they must use in prayer.
Romeo: O then, dear saint, let lips do what hands do;
    they pray, grant thou, lest faith turn to despair.
Juliet: Saints, do not move, though grant for prayers' sake.
Romeo: Then move not, while my prayer's effect I take.
    Thus from my lips by thine my sin is purged.
Juliet: Then have my lips the sin that they have took.
Romeo: Sin from my lips? O trespass sweetly urged
    Give me my sin again.

Every student yearned for some teenage beauty who would say of him, as Juliet said of Romeo:

    Give me my Romeo; and, when I shall die,
    Take him and cut him out in little stars,
    And he will make the face of heaven so fine,
    That all the world will be in love with night,
    And pay no worship to the garish sun.

For the campus as well as the country folk, Shakespeare would write *A Midsummer Night's Dream*, which, if it shines like *Romeo and Juliet*, shines not sadly but merrily. There is no death in *Midsummer Night's Dream*, and the smiling horizon is immeasurably remote. The play is a lover's fantasy.

In the Warwickshire of Shakespeare, belief in the fairy kingdom and the powers exercised by such spirits was general.[6] About such elves Shakespeare etched verse that would become music. The fairies become lovable. No wonder the composer Felix Mendelssohn would write the overture to *Midsummer Night's Dream*. Nick Bottom, the weaver in this fairy tale, says to the fairy queen Titania, "I have a reasonable good ear in music. Let's have the tongs and the bones."

Bottom takes an interest in the moon, if only among the pages of an almanac. "A calendar, a calendar!" He calls, "Find out moonshine, find out moonshine." And when they do, these Athenian mechanics, of whom he is king, are taken over by moonlight. If *Romeo and Juliet* is shot with stars, *A Midsummer Night's Dream* is drenched with moonlight.

For characters, Shakespeare would draw on the tradesmen he remembered from the streets of Stratford—a joiner, a weaver, a bellows-mender, and a tailor. It has been said that Shakespeare first had the idea of the play one June night in the village of Grendon, which has a charming inn that bears the sign of the Ship. (Grendon marks the first stage of the journey from Stratford to London.) There Shakespeare supposedly met a townsman who inspired the clownish character of Bottom, the hero of strange events brought about by Puck during that fantastic night.[7]

Yet Puck and the other fairies are not malevolent, only mischievous. Towards humans they are indifferently amused. "Lord, what fools these mortals be!" observes Puck.

Love is a form of madness in which Cupid "loosed his love-shaft smartly from his bow, as it should pierce a hundred thousand hearts."

For his next subject Shakespeare turned from elves to current events. Lopes, a Portuguese Jewish physician, had been prosecuted at the urging of Cecil, Elizabeth's chief counsellor, on the trumped-up charge of trying to poison the Queen. The doctor was executed in 1593. If anyone should doubt the connection between Shylock and Lopes, the description of Shylock as a wolf is the key. *Lopes* in Portuguese means wolf.[8]

> Thy currish spirit
> Govern'd a wolf, who hang'd for human slaughter,
> Even from the gallows did his fell soul fleet
> . . .
> for thy desires
> Are wol'ish, bloody, starved and ravenous.

As in the Dreyfus case in nineteenth-century France, Lopes had been the victim of anti-Semitic prejudice. Marlowe, in *The Jew of Malta*, had pandered to mob sentiment by bringing to stage the madman Barrabas, who tried to poison all London.

Shakespeare's *Merchant of Venice* is roughly patterned after the Marlowe play, but Shylock is not a monster. Shakespeare had little use for Cecil, Elizabeth's minister, and believed that Lopes had been framed. Because of public sentiment, he could not make the Jew a hero, but he did let the moneylender make a case for himself. Dustin Hoffman, in 1990, as many actors did in Victorian England, portrayed Shylock sympathetically as a wronged and suffering man. Shylock makes a compelling speech:

I am a Jew. Hath not a Jew eyes? hath not a Jew hands, organs, dimensions, senses, affections, passions? . . . If you prick us, do we not bleed? If you tickle us, do we not laugh? If you poison us, do we not die? and if you wrong us, shall we not revenge?

Shakespeare's Shylock is more victim than villain. He is not a beast, but a butt for audience laughter. He is a man thrust into a world bound not to tolerate him. Shylock is a lonely soul, and his isolation gives him a majesty denied to his garrulous foes, who are hardly heroes: "the bankrupt Antonio . . . a weakling without energy"; Bassanio, a true fortune hunter; and Lorenzo, the accomplice of an infamous burglary.

The only praiseworthy character is Portia. She is the first of Shakespeare's many strong heroines, in a day when women's parts were mostly minor roles, played by lads who were literally minors. In one of Shakespeare's most recited speeches, Portia, assuming the guise of a lawyer, wins freedom from the death penalty for her fiancé Antonio. The role must have challenged some young Burbage company performer—he had to play a woman playing a man. Portia's address is a combination of head and heart, a rational plea for mercy.

> The quality of mercy is not strain'd,
> It droppeth as the gentle rain from heaven
> Upon the place beneath: it is twice blessed;
> It blesseth him that gives, and him that takes:
> 'Tis mightiest in the mightiest; it becomes
> The throned monarch better than his crown.

When Shakespeare restructured Marlowe's play from tragedy to comedy, he created a part for Will Kempe, the chief comedian in the Burbage company.[9] Kempe would play the clownish servant Launcelot Gobbo, who leaves the employ of Shylock to work for Antonio. Kempe was a sandy-haired comic whose squat figure belied a nimble dexterity.[10] He had started his entertainment career as a carnival acrobat. This one-time dancer had perfected a two-step that bore his name, "the Kempe jig." He was an actor who could improvise lines as well as steps, and a juggler who could time an ad-lib to fit any gesture or grimace.[11]

Londoners came out to see Portia save her lover Bassanio, but the characters they remembered were Shylock the Jew and Gobbo the clown. Next Kempe would steal the show in *Midsummer Night's Dream*, as Bottom the weaver.[12] It had been the same with *Romeo and Juliet*. The students came to watch the plight of the lovers, but the actor who stole their affections was the clownish Peter, also played by Kempe.[13]

NOTES

1. S. Schoenbaum, *William Shakespeare* (New York: Oxford University Press, 1987), p. 159.

2. Joseph Quincy Adams, *A Life of William Shakespeare* (Boston: Houghton Mifflin, 1923), pp. 220–21.

The play won fame at the universities. In the recently discovered original Bodleian copy of the First Folio, which was chained to the shelves where it could be read by the students, the wear on the leaves shows that of all the plays of Shakespeare the one which most pleased the young man of the university was *Romeo and Juliet*.

3. Marquette Shute, *Shakespeare of London* (New York: Dutton, 1949), pp. 154–57.

4. Ibid., p. 157.

5. Adams, *Life of Shakespeare*, p. 222.

6. Peter Quennell, *Shakespeare: The Poet and His Background* (Cleveland: World, 1963), pp. 170–71.

7. Clara Longworth de Chambrun, *Shakespeare: A Portrait Restored* (London: Holis & Carter, 1957), p. 82.

8. Chambrun, *Shakespeare: Portrait*, p. 186.

9. Chambrun, *Shakespeare: Portrait*, p. 128; Peter Levi, *The Life and Times of William Shakespeare* (New York: Holt, 1988), p. 47; Schoenbaum, *William Shakespeare*, p. 184.

10. Chambrun, *Shakespeare: Portrait*, pp. 128–29; Levi, *Life and Times of Shakespeare*, p. 47.

11. Adams, *Life of Shakespeare*, p. 219; Quennell, *Shakespeare*, p. 149.

12. Adams, *Life of Shakespeare*, p. 219.

13. Shute, *Shakespeare of London*, p. 159.

CHAPTER NINE

Plague and Passion

Lust is but a bloody fire,
Kindled with unchaste desire.

Merry Wives of Windsor
act 5, scene 5

If Kempe and Richard Burbage had their growing claque of followers, Burbage's Theatre owed most of its new prosperity to Shakespeare, who had the Midas touch, turning old plots into fresh-minted, golden poetry. He had mastered the secrets of terror and tragedy, and broadened his range from chronicle to comedy.

Yet in 1593 the Theatre suddenly had to shut down, for a frightful reason. The plague, with its deadly swellings and fever, had struck, and by the early summer of 1594 the death toll had mounted from hundreds into thousands.

Anytime the death toll reached 500 in three weeks, "plague orders" automatically took effect. Under the regulations of the City Council, all performers, all exhibitions, all meetings were banned—be they circuses, bearbaitings, cockfights, or stage plays. The only place people could assemble was in church, where they crowded into the pews invoking God to spare their families.[1] Markets emptied; shops closed; businesses slumped—except for peddlers hawking magic elixirs to ward off the dreaded disease.

The plague came just as James Burbage had established his company as the premier stage group in London. Ten years previously plague orders had shut down the company. Burbage and his son Cuthbert, who was his deputy business manager, sent letters to outlying cities beyond the plague's reach, such as Bath, Bristol, and Exeter, to drum up a few engagements to keep the nucleus of the company together.[2] In provincial cities the company staged its plays in town halls or tavern yards after receiving the patronage of a local lord or earl. In the yards of inns, stages were crudely fashioned by putting planks over barrel heads.[3]

Shakespeare must have left his London lodgings for Stratford, and except for a few scattered engagements with the Burbage company in provincial cities, he would probably have stayed there. His daughter Susanna was now almost 10, and the twins Hamnet and Judith were 9. The fair-haired son and heir must have been a particular source of pride for Shakespeare, as well as for his wife Anne.

The family, which must have just eked by on Shakespeare's earnings as an actor, now could begin to enjoy the fruits of his success. No doubt the children had sorely missed their father, whose visits had usually been at Christmas and Easter, and on those occasions when performances at Oxford or Birmingham brought him to the general vicinity. For a while at least, the family was united.

At Stratford Shakespeare turned his pen from plays to poetry.[4] He put his hand to completing an epic poem that he may have begun years earlier—*Venus and Adonis*.[5] Shakespeare had learned Latin in school, and Ovid was his favorite poet. Ovid's *Ars Amatoria* (*The Art of Love*) was a particular favorite. Shakespeare's long poem is also about love.

But Shakespeare was not composing this poetry for the general public. In a real sense he was writing for one reader: Henry Wriothesley, the Earl of Southampton. For some time Shakespeare had been cultivating a friendship with the young earl.[6] Southampton was known as a patron of writers, including the scholar John Florio (his tutor in Italian) and the poet and dramatist Thomas Nash. In *Merchant of Venice* the comic character Kempe had played was Launcelot Gobbo; Gobbo was the actual name of a servant in the Southampton household.[7]

Just as playwrights today seek backers, or "angels," sponsors in Elizabethan days were called patrons. Theatrical entertainment in the sixteenth century, like cockfights and bearbaiting, was just about as illegal as speak-easies in the 1920s. Acting companies sought the sponsorship of the powerful, such as Lord Hunsdon, whose mother was a sister of Anne Boleyn, which made him a cousin of the Queen. Lord Hunsdon was lord chamberlain, and until 1603 Shakespeare's acting company was known as the Lord Chamberlain's Company.[8] It helped both players and playwrights to have a friend at Court.

The accepted method of wooing a potential patron was public praise in the form of poetry. This was almost like writing a prospectus for an investor. When Shakespeare came to London, he has to have known of Southampton—Southampton's father had been lord of the manor of Snitterfield, where Shakespeare's father had been born and his grandfather Richard Shakespeare worked as a tenant farmer.[9] Young Southampton was winning a reputation as the city's foremost young man-about-town. Yet if Southampton was a playboy, he must also have been brilliant, since he had entered St. John's College, Cambridge, at the age of 12, in 1585.[10]

Eight years younger than Shakespeare, Southampton was as rich as he was handsome. His dazzling jewels could compete with his golden curls. In the Van Dyck portrait in London we see Southampton wearing a thin satin doublet, with white trunks and knee breeches laced with gold. Garters of purple stitched with silver hold up his white stockings. Little white silk bows, like four-petaled flowers, decorate the sword belt. The sword hilt is overlaid with gold. His right hand, in an embroidered and jeweled gauntlet, rests by a white plumed helmet. A quick glance at the foppishly dressed Southampton suggests effeminacy, but on closer study one is struck by eyes of virile intensity.[11]

Southampton cut a wide swath in court circles, where his elegant presence delighted Queen Elizabeth. He and his friends frequently occupied his box in front of the stage at the Theatre.

Southampton fancied himself a connoisseur of the arts, but his most noteworthy artistic collection was of erotic poetry.[12] He was a libertine, and his womanizing caused him to be banished from Court when Queen Elizabeth learned that her lady-in-waiting Elizabeth Vernon would be bearing Southampton's child.

Before that Southampton had alienated the Queen's minister, Lord Cecil, by refusing to marry Elizabeth de Vere, Cecil's granddaughter. The de Veres were an old and powerful family; Elizabeth's father was the Earl of Oxford. For Southampton to snub the matchmaking was a slap at Cecil. After all, Cecil had helped Southampton enroll at Cambridge. Southampton's father, a partisan of Mary Stuart, had been jailed for treason and soon thereafter died, and Cecil, who had felt sorry for the orphaned son, had tried to look after Southampton.[13]

Shakespeare was not the only playwright seeking the patronage of Southampton. Christopher Marlowe, whose predilections were not heterosexual, was also dedicating works to this lord he professed to admire.

Today a young man coming to Washington might seek the help of his senator, or a senator his family knows. In Shakespeare's day the "Senate" was the House of Lords, and Shakespeare chose the young Southampton as the most likely candidate for his friend in Court. After all, Southampton's father had been the lord of the village where John Shakespeare grew up.

So Shakespeare sought to gain the attention of Southampton. To that purpose he wrote *Venus and Adonis*, as well as scores of sonnets. The theme of such sonnets was life or love. Some of his more familiar lines serve as an example.

> Shall I compare thee to a summer's day?
> Thou art more lovely and more temperate:
> Rough winds do shake the darling buds of May,
> And summer's lease hath all too short a date:
> . . .
> But thy eternal summer shall not fade,
> Nor lose possession of that fair thou owest.
>
> When to the sessions of sweet silent thought
> I summon up remembrance of things past,
> . . .
> Then can I drown an eye, unused to flow,
> For precious friends hid in death's dateless night.

If we had only his sonnets by which to remember Shakespeare, he might be remembered like an Andrew Marvell or perhaps a John Donne. It was his plays that would afford him expression of his nobility and complexity of character, which would translate into any language as well as into such other mediums as music and ballet.

We call Shakespeare the Bard, but he was first a businessman. He was self-made, just like his father John, who in 1593 was still struggling to regain the commercial success he had once enjoyed. The difference was in the products they sold: pairs of gloves and parcels of wool by the father; plays and poetry by the son.

Shakespeare wrote for money—and he would make it, a lot of it! No wonder some other playwrights resented him. They said he was not a scholar, yet Shakespeare made no pretense of being one. He was an actor; he knew what would entertain the public, and he served it up. Because of his ageless insights on human nature, the reader might envision Shakespeare as a larger-than-life literary titan like Count Tolstoy or George Bernard Shaw, but he was perhaps closer to the present-day Neil Simon in New York or Alan Ayckbourne in London. Perhaps Shakespeare would have been drawn to Hollywood. The masses he could reach, and the money he could make, would have been an irresistible lure for someone with his flair for fast script writing. Shakespeare saw himself as an actor who could adapt old plots into popular drama; he did not think of himself as a philosopher, but as an entertainer.

Shakespeare neither postured as a scholar nor pontificated as a philosopher. If he had been pressed about his talent, he might have admitted that he had a flair for turning old tales into exciting conflicts, with complex characters and quotable lines. It was a gift that would bring him money and position. Like so many other giants in history, Shakespeare was the right man at the right time. He came to London when English drama was first developing. Marlowe had opened the way with his tragedies, and Burbage had built his Theatre to stage them.

Winston Churchill, who died four centuries after Shakespeare's birth, was another giant of English history who would answer the need of a moment. Like Shakespeare, Churchill lacked a university degree, and like Shakespeare, Churchill wrote for profit. Shakespeare and Churchill were both conservatives in ideals, but romantics in imagination.[14] Peter Quennell writes, "He [Shakespeare] is a conservative, even a reactionary, an opponent of Raleigh's School and their subversive doctrines, a man whose lively intelligence does not seek to challenge the established order."[15] Shakespeare said in *King Lear*, "The lamentable change is from the best," and Churchill would later ask, "What is conservatism if not adherence to the old and the best."[16] Churchill and Shakespeare both spent most of their lives in London, but in their hearts they still regarded themselves as country squires. Virtuosity in their own language was the route both men would follow to success and fame.

Shakespeare, however, was a better businessman than Churchill. His profits from the Burbage company, as well as his payments for acting, he plowed into purchases of property in Warwickshire that enhanced his estate. Shakespeare would take in about £100 a year for his acting, £200 a year from his shares in the company, and about £15 for each play he wrote. He averaged some two or three plays a year, and he would receive bonuses for certain performances played at the request of the Queen.

Unlike Churchill, Shakespeare was not the grandson of a duke, but the son of a shopkeeper. Churchill would squander his earnings to live in the ducal style of his grandfather, while Shakespeare squirreled away his shillings to buy the land that would make him a country squire.

Shakespeare, like Churchill, wrote for a living. The poetry he was penning in his enforced idleness from the stage had a purpose: to win the backing of the powerful Earl of Southampton, who had influence at the court of Elizabeth. Like a modern businessman trying to interest a rich investor, Shakespeare was seeking to enlist Southampton's backing. His principal presentation in this effort would be *Venus and Adonis*. For the prudish, some of the passages might be labeled X-rated.

> I'll be a park, and thou shalt be my deer;
> Feed where thou wilt, on mountain or in dale:
> Graze on my lips, and if those hills be dry,
> Stray lower, where the pleasant fountains lie.

But the sonnets, which he continued to compose in his late twenties and early thirties, both before and after the plague, reflect a mixed purpose. At an inner level they reflected the passions of his personal life.

Shakespeare probably had fallen in love—except that it was more lust than love. The object of his obsession is known in history as the Dark Lady of the sonnets. Some scholars, such as Peter Levi, have identified her as Emilia Bassano Lanier, a musician's wife, who turned many an eye in the court of Queen Elizabeth. Emilia had been a mistress of Lord Hunsdon, the lord chamberlain. In 1592, when she became pregnant, Hunsdon then foisted her off in marriage to Captain Alfonso Lanier, a court musician.

From the sonnets we know that the Dark Lady was a coquette, whose assets included more than her ability to sing a song and play the lute. Emilia Lanier had quite a coterie of admirers in court circles, and their attentiveness was not diminished by her reputation for offering her favors for gifts of finery. The Bassanos were Jewish-Italian silk merchants, and the complexion of the Dark Lady would coincide with such a Mediterranean background. We can well imagine that her sultry looks and provocative figure were the object of masculine fantasies.

If Shakespeare was entranced by the voluptuous Mrs. Lanier, he was not alone. She later caught the eye of the womanizing Southampton. Perhaps Southampton had become intrigued by Shakespeare's sonnets, which so glowingly describe the charms of the seductive Emilia. Shakespeare's reaction is expressed when he laments:

> O how faint when I of you do write
> Knowing a better spirit doth use your name.

The Dark Lady of the sonnets toyed with Shakespeare's affections, then apparently shifted her attention from the protégé to his patron. Shakespeare knew he could not compete with the richer Southampton:

> Farewell thou art too dear for my possessing
> And like enough thou know'st thy estimate

Southampton was not only younger, but had more money, as well as more status and power. So between this young earl and his older protégé glides the shadow of a dark and sensual woman, the poet's mistress, who seduces his friend and whose treachery he accepts in a mood of masochistic resolution, only begging that despite his enslavement, she will not deprive him of his second self.[17]

> So now I have confessed that he is thine
> And I myself am mortgaged to thy will
> Myself I'll forfeit, so that other mine
> Thou wilt restore to be my comfort still
> But thou will not, nor he will not be free
> For thou art covetous and he is kind
> He learn'd but surety, like to write for me
> Under that hand that him as fast doth bind.

Shakespeare hinted at the Dark Lady's inconstancy with these lines:

> How sweet and lovely dost thou make the shame
> Which like a canker in the fragrant rose,
> Doth spot the beauty of thy budding name!
> O, in what sweets dost thy sins enclose!

The situation between Shakespeare and Southampton might have been not just a triangle but a double triangle. Shakespeare and Southampton could have been both wooing Emilia, while at a literary level Shakespeare and Marlowe were bidding for Southampton's patronage.

The bachelor Marlowe might have been gaining the upper hand, but he would die on May 30, 1593, of a knife-stabbing in a tavern in Deptford. Some say that Marlowe's enemies put out the story that he was murdered by a rival, jealous of Marlowe's attentions to the killer's homosexual lover. Today, however, some scholars believe Marlowe was assassinated.[18] While he was attending Corpus Christi, Cambridge, Marlowe had joined the English secret service, the elaborate system of counterespionage developed by Cecil's deputy Sir Francis Walsingham. As a spy, Marlowe would pose as a Catholic convert to collect intelligence, and then report on the Catholic sympathizers to Cecil.[19]

Such an assassination might have colored Shakespeare's words in *Titus Andronicus*: "I must talk of murders, . . . acts of black night, abominable deeds, complots of mischief, treason, villanies, ruthful to hear, yet piteously performed." Marlowe's death, however, left an undisputed king of English playwrights—William Shakespeare.

NOTES

1. Joseph Quincy Adams, *A Life of William Shakespeare* (Boston: Houghton Mifflin, 1923), pp. 108–10; S. Schoenbaum, *William Shakespeare* (New York: Oxford University Press, 1987), pp. 167–69.

2. Marquette Shute, *Shakespeare of London* (New York: Dutton, 1949), p. 105.

3. Ibid., pp. 25–27.

4. Adams, *Life of Shakespeare*, pp. 145–56.

5. Ibid., pp. 148–50.

6. Ibid., p. 151.

7. Clara Longworth de Chambrun, *Shakespeare: A Portrait Restored* (London: Holis & Carter, 1957), p. 187.

8. Peter Quennell, *Shakespeare: The Poet and His Background* (Cleveland: World, 1963), p. 164; Peter Levi, *The Life and Times of William Shakespeare* (New York: Holt, 1988), pp. 40–41.

9. Levi, *Life and Times of Shakespeare*, p. 10.

10. Schoenbaum, *William Shakespeare*, pp. 170–71.

11. Quennell, *Shakespeare*, p. 117.

12. Adams, *Life of Shakespeare*, p. 153.

13. Chambrun, *Shakespeare: Portrait*, p. 97.

14. Tucker Brooke, *Shakespeare of Stratford* (New Haven, Conn.: Yale University Press, 1926), p. 144.

15. Quennell, *Shakespeare*, p. 147.

16. Winston Churchill, Speech before the Conservative Party Conference, 1955.

17. Quennell, *Shakespeare*, pp. 129–30.

18. Quennell, *Shakespeare*, pp. 47–49.

19. Ibid.

CHAPTER TEN

The Plot and the Play

Let us assay our plot.

All's Well that Ends Well
act 3, scene 7

Besides himself, Southampton most adored Robert Devereux, the Earl of Essex. The gallant and popular Essex had also become the Queen's favorite, though 25 years her junior. The Earl of Essex was every bit as handsome as Southampton, but he was more soldier than sport, more politician than playboy. He wanted to be king, and much of England would have welcomed him.

One who opposed Essex was William Cecil, the Baron of Burghley, who was the Queen's chief minister and the state treasurer. Some of those behind Cecil were called Puritans. Puritans were trying to label those championing the cause of Essex as Papists, and certainly Essex, whose family included many of the "old religion," was somewhat sympathetic to the Catholics.

Southampton too despised the Puritans. His early memories were of the persecution of his father for his overtures to Mary Queen of Scots, a Catholic.

As for Cecil, he saw Catholicism as a threat to the English throne. He may have offered a friendly ear to the low-church partisans, but what really mattered to him was not Puritanism but power. So a struggle erupted between Cecil, who was virtually the Queen's prime minister, and Essex, the Queen's supposed paramour.

Cecil had more friends in Court, but Essex, a charismatic figure with dashing charm, was more popular with the people. But if Essex had the good looks of a John Kennedy, Cecil had the craftiness and experience of a Richard Nixon, but aging, and with the gout.[1]

The Queen used her sex to manipulate the Court. To overcome the disadvantage of being a woman ruler in the male world of the Court, she played a double role of divine majesty and earthly woman. It was a shrewd ploy; if her gender was the problem, it was also the solution. She shamelessly flirted with the courtiers and mercilessly toyed with their emotions. Essex was dazzled by the Queen, and he knew that Elizabeth loved him. Yet he never quite knew where he stood with this imperious and capricious woman, whose moods changed as rapidly as the English clouds cover and uncover the sun.

In 1930 the play *Elizabeth and Essex* would be made into a movie. Errol Flynn would portray the swashbuckling Essex, and Bette Davis, Elizabeth. In real life the balding Elizabeth was closer to ugly than beautiful. Her white face was shriveled into wrinkles, and her teeth were blackened by that new delicacy, sugar, which she constantly nibbled at. Rouge and paint could not disguise the lines, nor could an outlandish reddish wig deflect attention from the ravages of age. Yet still she radiated the majesty of a queen.

Essex did little to conceal his exits from the Queen's boudoir in the early hours of the morning. If the affair was never actually consummated, then both of them were pretending otherwise. Vanity led Elizabeth to carry on the charade, while for Essex the relationship offered access to the throne. Eventually Essex tired of being Elizabeth's pet, however. He wanted power.[2]

For Essex to win, he needed to trigger the English people into action. As a lieutenant to Essex, Lord Southampton thought a new play by Shakespeare might light the fuse.[3] Shakespeare had an idea: What if he picked as his next subject the story of Richard II, the king who was dethroned by the soldier Henry Bolingbroke? As a woman, Elizabeth was, in a sense, a more vulnerable monarch than Richard II. As Peter Quennell writes in his biography of Shakespeare, "The fall of Richard II haunted the Queen's mind."[4] The fate of Richard II, who is "surrounded by a thousand flatterers," was not lost on Elizabeth.

In 1594 Shakespeare must have been a frequent visitor to Holborn House, the London residence of Southampton. Shakespeare, who might also have acted as a sometime tutor for Southampton's family, had now solidified himself as the earl's protégé.

Shakespeare had already presented *Venus and Adonis*, "the first heir of my invention, . . . to the Right Honourable Henry Wriothesley, Earl of

Southampton and Baron of Titchfield." Southampton had been delighted. The London sport could now boast that the finest erotic poetry since Ovid was dedicated to him.

When the poem was distributed to the public, it was a rage with young gentlemen, particularly those in the universities. An author of a play at Cambridge University at the time has one of the students exclaim, "Let this duncified world esteem of Spenser and Chaucer: I'll worship sweet Mister Shakespeare and to honor him will lay his *Venus and Adonis* under my pillow."

The spring of 1595 in London lifted not only the chill of winter but the pall of the plague. During the winter months Shakespeare had finished *King Richard II*. The play must have been the result of months of effort; no other chronicle or tragedy packs so great a proportion of poetry to prose. Only his comedies have more rhyming verse. Shakespeare in later years would depend less on rhyme and more on imagery expressed in blank verse, but he had reason to resort to rhyme in *Richard II*. To the illiterate penny public, rhymes were what catchy lyrics are today: they remained in the mind. If Essex wanted the play to rouse the masses, some of the dialogue had to become popular slogans.

In addition, Shakespeare loaded the script with holy phrases by referring to the Bible. Two bibles were in use in those days. The Bishop's Bible was the one the clergy read in church. The Geneva Bible, however, was the bible of the people, complete with annotations and commentary. This, of course, was more than just the most widely read book of its day—it was the guide for life. The many references to the Holy Scripture in *Richard II* added power to the play's message and sanctity to the dialogue.

The audience would hear allusions to Abel, "Mary's Son," "Three Judases," Eve, what "Judas did to Jesus," Pilate, Cain, and the field of Golgotha. In the first scene Norfolk tells Richard that one cannot change the leopard's spots, alluding to a verse in Jeremiah. Shakespeare even has Richard, in his final dungeon hours, quote exactly from the Geneva text:

> As thus, "Come little ones," and then again,
> "It is as hard to come as for a camel
> To thread the postern of a small needle's eye."

Shakespeare showed the final product to James Burbage, but the practical manager saw one insurmountable problem. In no way could a play in which a reigning monarch is deposed slip past the Master of Revels, who was the government censor at Court.[5] Shakespeare had probably already worked on one play that was stopped by censors. A play about the martyred Sir Thomas More, which many scholars think Shakespeare was a collaborator in, was banned by the ministers of the Queen, whose father, Henry VIII, had ordered the saintly servant of the Crown executed. (The story of More would help inspire Robert Bolt to write *A Man for All Seasons* four centuries later).[6]

What worried Burbage was remarks about abdication by Richard II to Henry Bolingbroke, the usurper of his throne. Some have suggested that Shakespeare himself played the role of "gentle Richard" against Burbage's Bolingbroke. At any rate, it is a delight to imagine Shakespeare at 30, slender and dignified in his role as the young king, voicing in rhyme the abdication to the burly Burbage as Bolingbroke:

> You may my glories and my state depose.
> But all my griefs; still I am king of those.

The company's solution to the problem was simple, if sly—they would delete the passage from the script that was sent to the censor. Actors like Shakespeare and Burbage, though, did not need a script to remember the seditious lines when they appeared on stage. Some of the acting company must have worried about acting in a play that would risk a monarch's wrath.

In the situation she faced, Elizabeth may have been as vulnerable as young Richard II had been two centuries before. But where the Plantagenet ruler had been impulsive and irresolute, the Tudor queen was manipulative and determined.

In his comparative sketches of Richard and his antagonist, the exiled Bolingbroke, Shakespeare serves up a manual on monarchy. To Richard the crown is a problem, but to Bolingbroke it is a prize. Richard notes Bolingbroke's playing to public opinion with mixed feelings of envy and disdain:

> Observed his courtship to the common people
> How did he seem to dive into their hearts
> With humble and familiar courtesy
> What reverence did he throw away on slaves
> Wooing poor craftsmen with the craft of smiles.

Richard II is a concerto for a poet who happens to be a king, sweetened with exquisite melodies for Richard's solo violin. The poet-king tries to prod himself:

I had forgot myself: am I not King?
Awake, thou coward majesty! Thou sleepest.

Shakespeare crafts for Richard a fine battle speech invoking the divine
right of kings.

Not all the water in the rough rude sea
Can wash the balm off from an anointed king;
The breath of worldly men cannot depose
The deputy elected by the Lord:
For every man that Bolingbroke hath press'd
To lift shrewd steel against our golden crown,
God for his Richard hath in heavenly pay
A glorious angel: then, if angels fight,
Weak men must fall, for heaven still guards the right.

His adviser Salisbury tells him, though, that his call for support may be
too late.

O, call back yesterday, bid time return
And thou shalt have twelve thousand fighting men!

Yet when the defeated Richard sees his crown slipping from his grasp
into the reach of Bolingbroke, he says to his foe:

Well you deserve: they well deserve to have,
That know the strong'st and surest way to get.

Richard is admitting that those who do not command history become
its victims. The dying John of Gaunt, the father of the banished Bolingbroke, had foreseen the downfall of this gentle king, whose nature was
dreamy and dilatory. As Gaunt observed, "There is no virtue like necessity," which is a poetic version of the baseball manager Leo Durocher's
remark, "Nice guys finish last."

Richard had thought that once the Archbishop put the crown on his head
it was his forever, by right of divinity and descent. The Stalins of the world
would ask in reply, "The Pope! How many divisions has *he* got?"

A leader who is both headstrong and weak in purpose does not survive;
Richard would lose not only his throne but his life. Yet in the Tower prison
before his death, he displays a nobility not evident when he was king. In
his new self-knowledge, he recognizes his former posturing and admits

that, without a crown, he has nothing to recommend himself: "I wasted time, and now time doth waste me." Jeremy Irons, who has played Richard II, compared his portrayal to the peeling of an onion. As he is forced to shed his pretense and shallow values, the true core of the young Plantagenet king is revealed.

If *Richard II* were played in court, Queen Elizabeth would have watched with dread the abdication of the King. She would have pondered on Richard's reliance on divine right. Her own royal descent was more circuitous than celestial. She was the daughter of a king's second wife after divorce—a love match that had ended on the gallows when her mother, Anne Boleyn, was executed. Elizabeth had had to rely on her wits, not on doctrine.

On the other hand, her erstwhile favorite, Essex, rejoiced in the idea of dethronement. Essex also would flaunt his connection to the play. In the provincial cities he would come on stage in full armor to acknowledge the cheers of his growing group of followers.

The play was a hit for the Burbage company, but it did not result in success for Essex. The grateful Southampton is said to have shown his appreciation to the playwright by helping Shakespeare buy an estate manor for his father.[7] Now the Shakespeare family ambition for a coat of arms might at last be realized. A roustabout actor was on his way to becoming a gentleman.

NOTES

1. Peter Quennell, *Shakespeare: The Poet and His Background* (Cleveland: World, 1963), pp. 107–10.

2. Ibid., p. 109.

3. Marquette Shute, *Shakespeare of London* (New York: Dutton, 1949), pp. 248–49.

4. Quennell, *Shakespeare*, p. 198.

5. S. Schoenbaum, *William Shakespeare* (New York: Oxford University Press, 1987), p. 214.

6. Clara Longworth de Chambrun, *Shakespeare: A Portrait Restored* (London: Holis & Carter, 1957), p. 71.

7. Quennell, *Shakespeare*, pp. 166–67; Joseph Quincy Adams, *A Life of William Shakespeare* (Boston: Houghton Mifflin, 1923), p. 154.

CHAPTER ELEVEN

A Young Heir's Death

I will instruct my sorrows to be proud;
For grief is proud and makes his owner stoop.

King John
act 3, scene 1

In 1596 John Shakespeare was awaiting the answer to his petition for a coat of arms. The son, no less than the father, must have been eager for news from the Heralds' College in London.[1] The status of gentleman was perhaps even more advantageous to the son, in the disreputable profession of acting, than to the father, in the respectable trade of a merchant.

Those in power would have little objection to giving a coat of arms, and the rank it embodied, to a worthy, even if illiterate, shopkeeper. Yet the more established gentry resisted the social aspirations of shopkeepers and others in trade. Many in the new middle classes were puritan.[2] Those inclined toward puritan precepts might endorse raising a merchant to the rank of gentleman, but they would balk at elevating an actor. To call a performing vagabond a gentleman was a profanation—even if the actor was a servant of the Lord Chamberlain's acting company.

Yet just when it was learned that the Heralds' College in London was about to grant John Shakespeare's petition for his coat of arms, his grandson, the male heir Hamnet, became gravely ill. Perhaps he fell victim to the "swamp fever" that frequently emanated from the lowlands near Stratford. The 11-year-old Hamnet would die before word of his critical condition could be sent to the town of Kent, more than 100 miles away, where Shakespeare was performing with the Burbage company.[3]

Shakespeare, who wanted distinction for the Shakespeare name, now knew that the name would end with his own life. Even though he was among the first actors to qualify as gentlemen, the award he sought and gained had turned to ashes. The exquisite irony must not have been lost on such an accomplished playwright.

In grief Shakespeare plunged himself into writing a new play. His subject was King John. This Plantagenet king was as far removed from Shakespeare's time as Shakespeare is from ours. Arguably John was the worst and most unpopular king in England's history; today we remember him as the king who was forced by the English barons to accept the Magna Charta in 1215. In his relations abroad John was just as irresolute, and this is the focus of Shakespeare's play. In *King John* Shakespeare explores the sacrifice of principle in a world of power politics.

Like his Richard II, John is a weak man who compensates for effeteness with expediency and masks his cowardice with cruelty. To appease France, he sacrifices his nephew Arthur's life and sells the Prince's property in France. He shrugs off his opportunism with a maxim worthy of Machiavelli, "How oft the sight of means to do ill deeds makes ill deeds done."

King Philip of France, at the urging of the Vatican, breaks the treaty, and Pandulph, the emissary of the Pope, blesses the perfidy:

> The truth is then most done not doing it;
> . . .
> thou dost swear only to be forsworn.

Pandulph is an oily Ribbentrop, who would be comfortable with Hitler's remark, "Treaties are like pie crusts—made to be broken."

The play would be a chronicle, but also a vehicle for expressing love of country. Shakespeare was a patriot, and his love for England was never better expressed than in the closing words by Philip Faulconbridge, "the Bastard":

> This England never did, nor never shall,
> Lie at the proud foot of a conqueror,
> But when it first did help to wound itself.
> Now these her princes are come home again,
> Come the three corners of the world in arms,
> And we shall shock them. Nought shall make us rue,
> If England to itself do rest but true.

At a time when England still feared invasion from Spain, Faulconbridge's speech struck a chord with his countrymen. The penny public must have cheered the Bastard's defiant words. Philip, the only hero in this chronicle, was probably played to the penny public by Richard Burbage as swashbuckling Robin Hood. In an ironic twist to the illegitimacy of his birth, the Bastard is a model of what a rightful and resolute king would be. He is valorous, when his cousin the King is venal. Faulconbridge is disgusted by the amorality practiced by rulers:

> I am amazed, methinks, and lose my way
> Among the thorns and dangers of this world.

In the Bastard's magnificent speech on "commodity," Shakespeare generalizes about the way considerations of money warp policy. In Elizabethan times, "commodity" in its narrowest sense was the percentage paid on a loan or the profit to the lender, but in a larger sense it meant expediency, the exploitation of one's self-interest. The Bastard denounces his own king's appeasement and his sacrifice of principle to profit.

> That broker that still breaks the pate of faith
> That daily break-vow, he that wins of all
> Of Kings, of beggars, old men, young men, maids.
> . . . Commodity, the bias of the world . . .
> And this same bias, this Commodity
> This bawd, this broker, this all changing-word
> Clapped on the outward eye of fickle France
> Hath drawn him from his own determined aid
> From a resolved and honourable war
> To a most base and vile-concluded peace.

If the Bastard, like Churchill, rails against the appeasement policies of the British government, the Bastard also adds a private cynical comment:

> And why rail I on this Commodity
> But for he hath not wooed me yet.

But if love of country was a popular theme in *King John*, Shakespeare also etched a personal and deeper love. Prince Arthur in *King John* dies at age 11, the same age as his son Hamnet, who had been buried in Stratford on August 11th, 1596.[4] In the lines of Constance, the mother of the boy Arthur, we hear Shakespeare express his own grief:

> Grief fills the room up of my absent child,
> Lies in his bed, walks up and down with me
> Puts on his pretty looks, repeats his words,
> Remembers me of all his gracious parts,
> Stuffs out his vacant garments with his form.

Constance tells her priest:

> Father cardinal, I have heard you say
> That we shall see and know our friends in heaven:
> If that be true, I shall see my boy again.

In those poignant lines, Shakespeare is offering his own prayer. *King John* is a study in grief as well as government.

NOTES

1. Tucker Brooke, *Shakespeare of Stratford* (New Haven, Conn.: Yale University Press, 1926), p. 15.

2. Peter Quennell, *Shakespeare: The Poet and His Background* (Cleveland: World, 1963), p. 160. Stephen Gosset, the Puritan poet, mocked actors' social ambitions in 1582.

> England affords these glorious vagabonds
> That carried carst their fardels on their backs
> Couriers to ride on through the gazing streets
> Swooping it in their glaring satin suits.
>
> *The Return from Parnassus* (1595)

3. Marquette Shute, *Shakespeare of London* (New York: Dutton, 1949), p. 183.

4. Quennell, *Shakespeare*, pp. 160–61.

CHAPTER TWELVE

The Fat Falstaff

> Falstaff sweats to death,
> And lards the lean earth as he walks along.
>
> *I King Henry IV*
> act 2, scene 2

As the last decade of the century was beginning, Shakespeare must not have had enough hours in the day to do justice to all his duties as actor, director, and script writer. He worked every waking hour, performing in the afternoon and writing new plays in the morning and evening. The next drama would also be a chronicle, beginning where *Richard II* had ended.

As a playwright, Shakespeare may have found that turning another Holinshed chapter into verse was not the challenge it once had been. Instead, he wanted to turn "documentary" into drama. It was the development of characters, not chronicles, that now absorbed his interest.

In the Henry IV plays we see Shakespeare take the soldier Bolingbroke from *Richard II* and turn him into a more complex figure under the pressures of monarchy. He cannot forget dethroning his predecessor. In *II Henry IV* he tells Prince Hal:

> God knows, my son,
> By what by paths and indirect crook'd ways
> I met this crown; and I myself know well
> How troublesome it sat upon my head.

Earlier in the play the King expresses the weight of office more succinctly: "Uneasy lies the head that wears a crown." By Shakespeare's pen, the intrepid captain has become an introspective king.

Henry IV is yet a ruler who understands that he owes it to his subjects to kindle their loyalty by communicating his policies and plans:

> It never yet did hurt
> To lay down likelihoods and forms of hopes.

Remember, King Henry IV was not that well known to English audiences. American audiences today would know more about President John Adams than English audiences knew about Henry IV. Yet to the penny public the background of Henry IV might be interesting, as long as it was filled with the ringing clash of battle. Today we see how historic personages in televised miniseries on the U.S. Revolution or Civil War often come off as wooden. Shakespeare, however, would weld the political commentator's insight and the dramatist's imagination to make these remote kings take on flesh and soul.

When King Henry advises his son to wage a war abroad to shore up his lagging popularity, Shakespeare reveals the cynicism of power:

> Be it thy course to busy giddy minds
> With foreign quarrels; that action hence borne out
> May waste the memory of former days.

Yet it is the alienation of father from son that inspires an oft-quoted line. By the King's deathbed at the end of the two-part play, his son Prince Hal says, "I never thought to hear you speak again." King Henry replies: "Thy wish was father, Harry, to that thought."

A play that was just about the dour Henry Bolingbroke as king would bore audiences, so Shakespeare offered up the contrast of the King's son, Prince Hal, to Hotspur. One brief reference in Holinshed to the waywardness of the king's first son was enough to ignite the playwright's imagination. By Shakespeare's pen the restless prince becomes a playboy. Then, as a comparison to the irresponsible Hal, Shakespeare created Hotspur, a fleshed-out version of Faulconbridge in *King John*. Hotspur would be the swashbuckling knight that every "penny knave" standee yearned to be.

There had been a soldier in the (Catholic) Percy family who bore the nickname of Hotspur; in *I Henry IV* Shakespeare etches the soldier's character to fit the sobriquet. The poet might have been influenced by the fact that the Percy family was kin to his sponsor Southampton.[1] What is attractive in Hotspur is not so much that he is a brave knight who leads a revolt against Henry IV, but rather his volatility, which triggers the valor. When Hotspur is warned about his reckless undertaking against the King, he shrugs:

> O the blood more stirs
> To rouse a lion than to start a hare!

As an impatient captain, contemptuous of ideas or intellect, Hotspur is a kind of Hamlet in reverse: all action, no thought. But as a soldier, he has a charisma of command that the student Hamlet lacks. He is cocksure, and he thinks his courage is contagious. When Glendower says, "I can call spirits from the vasty deep," Hotspur replies, "Why so can I or so can any man, but will they come when you do call for them?"

While King Henry can admire Hotspur for his bravery, he regards his behavior as irresponsible in a leader:

> Defect of manners, want of government
> Pride, haughtiness, opinion and disdain
> The least of which haunting a nobleman
> Loses men's hearts.

He senses the defects that will lead to Hotspur's demise. Hotspur is later slain in battle by the King's son Prince Hal, but the credit for the killing is claimed by a bragging buffoon named Sir John Falstaff.

In all English literature there is no character that invites more affectionate amusement than Falstaff. He was invented long before Dickens, yet his is a Dickensian personality. Indeed, neither Pickwick nor Macawber would ever gain such a humorous purchase in the sentiments of English readers. Yet what was Falstaff? A cheat, a liar, a thief, a coward, a lecher, a glutton!

Shakespeare had broken new ground in literature. Not only had he introduced a comic character in a serious chronicle, but he had made what should have been a villain a favorite of audiences. Some might compare Falstaff in magnitude and texture to Don Quixote, whom Cervantes created for Spanish literature at about the same time. But that quaint tilter against windmills had virtues, while Falstaff had only vices and venality. When Falstaff's thieving habits are challenged, the fat squire answers, "Why, Hal, 'tis my vocation, Hal; 'tis no sin for a man to labour in his vocation."

Actually, the vocation of Sir John was that of a "military squire." In his day Shakespeare must have seen county commanders like Falstaff press the local misfits, ne'er-do-wells, and town drunks into a semblance of a militia to serve some earl or prince. Such a squire, along with his rag-tag assembly of soldiers, would receive little welcome from villagers, except in the local taverns.

Yet for all his self-indulgence, Falstaff has an earthy realism the audience could appreciate. It was as if Shakespeare in the various characters of Henry IV was sketching a composite for leadership that Prince Hal could learn from. His father had the prudence necessary, even though it was too burdened by guilt. Hotspur had the idealism, but neither the knowledge nor the temperament suited for government ("defect of manners, want of government.") The combination of Henry IV's caution, Hotspur's courage, and Falstaff's practicality would make an ideal king.

Falstaff was a tailor-made role for the Burbage company's comic star, Will Kempe. It has been suggested that Kempe might have said to Shakespeare, "Will, if you can shake a pen as well as you can shake a spear, we'll strike a deal." If so, Shakespeare more than lived up to the agreement. Kempe, with a pillow stuck in his belt to add some girth, would enjoy his greatest role. Falstaff would do for Will Kempe what Richard III had done for Richard Burbage.[2]

In the tight fraternity of actors, Kempe and Richard Burbage were Shakespeare's favorite companions. The prankish Kempe appealed to Shakespeare's playful side. If Shakespeare's sense of humor was ironic, that of Kempe was irrepressible. This dexterous barrel of man was both acrobat and actor, and his antics on the stage cannot be visualized in script. One cannot see his pratfalls or his lurching drunken gait, nor hear his belches and snores. Kempe did not have to say a word to steal a scene: when he entered on stage, the audience would laugh at the mere sight of him.

When playing the lovable lecher and cowardly captain, Kempe dwarfed the stage. W. C. Fields in the 1920s, Oliver Hardy in the 1940s, Bob Hope in the 1960s, and Jackie Gleason in the 1960s, owed much to the character of Falstaff, which Shakespeare painted and Kempe portrayed.

Curiously, the character would have been known as Sir John Oldcastle if not for the intervention of the Privy Council. William Brooke, the Lord Cobham, was Queen Elizabeth's Lord Chamberlain and descendant of the real Sir John Oldcastle.[3] As a young soldier, Oldcastle had been a drunkard and a glutton, but he was "born again" as a Puritan in later life. "Oldcastle" was the original name in Shakespeare's script, but under orders

Shakespeare changed John Oldcastle to John Fastolfe, who had figured as a coward in *I Henry VI*.

> Here had the conquest fully been sealed up
> If Sir John Fastolfe had not played the coward.

Falstaff is such a giant in literature that "Falstaffian" has passed into the English language as an adjective. One wonders how Oldcastle could have been made into an adjective!

Despite the change of name, Shakespeare found a way to signal to his audience that Falstaff is still a reference to Cecil's late brother-in-law, Oldcastle. When Falstaff comes on stage, Prince Hal greets him as "Falstaff, my old lad of the castle."[4]

Shakespeare and Kempe must have enjoyed their little laugh at the expense of the stiff and sober-minded Cecil. The ebullient Kempe brought out the impish side of Shakespeare, and the playwright used Falstaff to bring out the playful nature of Prince Hal.

Falstaff is a lovable rogue whose bravado belies his cowardice. Just before a battle in Part I, Prince Hal, the foil for Falstaff's most outlandish statements, tells the fearful Falstaff that bravery is a matter of honor, to which Falstaff blusters:

Can honour set to a leg? No. Or an arm? No. Or take away the grief of a wound? No. Honour hath no skill in surgery, then? No. What is honour? A word. What is that word, honour? Air. A trim reckoning!

Falstaff was such a hit that Shakespeare had to write a sequel, *Henry IV, Part II*. Not only did those in the penny pits embrace Falstaff in their affections, but royalty as well. The Queen liked it so much that she ordered Shakespeare to write in two weeks a play just about Falstaff for the next feast day, which was that of Saint George[5] (which, of course, was also Shakespeare's birthday). The Queen specifically requested that Shakespeare have the philandering Falstaff fall in love.[6]

If the deadline was two weeks, it was too short a time even for the fast-writing Shakespeare to dash off a play in blank verse. Even if he wrote it in one week, the actors would only have another week to learn the lines. How could he meet the royal deadline? Out of necessity, he discarded poetry for prose. How could he get away with that? Simple: he would write a comedy about common folk. It was an accepted conceit of Elizabethan drama that only the gentry spoke in iambic pentameter. So Shakespeare would write a play about everyday villagers.

Shakespeare set the play in Windsor, where stood the country castle of Queen Elizabeth. We know the play as *The Merry Wives of Windsor*, the only comedy situated in England and written in prose. But though the town was called Windsor, it was really Stratford.

The characters were drawn from his boyhood in Stratford. There was Mistress Quickly, the bawdy busybody, and Pistol, the town oracle. As mentioned in Chapter 1, Sir Hugh Evans, the stern Welsh parson, was based on the Thomas Jenkins who had once drilled Shakespeare in Latin.

In the play, teacher Evans quizzes a pupil named William:

Evans: What is he that does lend articles?
William: Articles are borrowed of the pronoun, and be thus declined: *Singulariter, nominatius, hic, haec, hoc* . . .
Evans: What is your genitive case plural, William?
William: Genitive case?
Evans: Ay.
William: Genitive—*horum, harum, horum.*

Since Shakespeare was really writing about his home town, he could not leave out the judge who had persecuted his family. Shallow is a parody of the family nemesis, Sir Thomas Lucy, who, it will be recalled, fined Shakespeare's father for not attending church and may have apprehended Shakespeare himself for poaching a deer. If so, Shallow's name suggests Lucy's lack of depth in his religious convictions, as evidenced by his shift from Protestant to Catholic and back to Protestant to fit the changing politics of the Court.

Shallow comes to Windsor still bewailing Falstaff's poaching and claiming he will take the knight to the highest court, which was the Star Chamber. Justice Shallow is assisted by his obsequious cousin Slender. Just as Shallow is modeled on Lucy, Slender is patterned after William Wayte, who in real life was a cousin of Lucy's and wore on his doublet the Lucy coat of arms.[7]

Wayte had tried to stop Shakespeare's company from acting one winter, claiming the play and performers were a threat to public morality. When Shakespeare legally blocked his move, Wayte lied, saying that Shakespeare had threatened to have him beaten up. For Shakespeare, the gentlest of men, this charge was ludicrous. Though he lived in an age of violence, no fistfight or threat of duel is recorded in Shakespeare's life, while Wayte had a record of blackmail, extortions, and frauds. Shakespeare, no doubt, chose the surname "Slender," as an ironic contrast to "Wayte" (weight).[8]

The general theme of *Merry Wives of Windsor* is simple: Falstaff meets two handsome married women and thinks he will make an easy conquest of both. "Briefly, I do mean to make love to Ford's wife: I spy entertainment in her; . . . She gives the leer of invitation." But gay Mistress Ford and beautiful Mistress Page are mindful of the maxim, "Wives may be merry and honest too." Falstaff at the end says "I do begin to perceive that I am made an ass."

After the Henry IV plays and *Merry Wives of Windsor*, Falstaff was so popular that Shakespeare had a problem. He could see that if it was left up to the penny public, not to mention Will Kempe, he might spend the rest of his life writing about the larger-than-life rogue. Other authors, like Sir Arthur Conan Doyle, have been in the same predicament. And Shakespeare chose the same way out that Doyle took with Sherlock Holmes: he had Falstaff die behind the scenes in his next play, *Henry V.*

NOTES

1. Clara Longworth de Chambrun, *Shakespeare: A Portrait Restored* (London: Holis & Carter, 1957), pp. 189–90.

2. Joseph Quincy Adams, *A Life of William Shakespeare* (Boston: Houghton Mifflin, 1923), pp. 226–27.

3. Ibid., pp. 228–29.

4. Chambrun, *Shakespeare: Portrait*, pp. 191–92; Peter Quennell, *Shakespeare: The Poet and His Background* (Cleveland: World, 1963), p. 204; Marquette Shute, *Shakespeare of London* (New York: Dutton, 1949), pp. 174–75; Adams, *Life of Shakespeare*, pp. 228–29.

5. Adams, *Life of Shakespeare*, pp. 232–33.

6. Ibid.

7. Shute, *Shakespeare of London*, p. 235.

8. Ibid.

CHAPTER THIRTEEN

Help for a Hero

Upon your sword
Sit laurel victory! and smooth success
Be strew'd before your feet!

Antony and Cleopatra
act 1, scene 3

Meanwhile, Shakespeare's patron, the Earl of Southampton, was having his own problems. His friend Essex had his back to the wall in Ireland. Though he seemed a reluctant participant, Southampton tried to help by leading a flotilla to Cadiz, which would block the Spanish navy from reinforcing the Irish leader Tyrone. Yet it was not Tyrone who was running out of supplies, but Essex. For neither the first nor the last time in the tangled history of those two countries, the English occupation of Ireland ran into trouble. The failure was not wholly the fault of Essex.

When Essex volunteered to Elizabeth to lead the invasion of Ireland, Cecil shrewdly raised no objection to the appointment. Then, as state treasurer, and without his sovereign's knowledge, Cecil held back on sending the reinforcements Essex needed to complete the conquest.

The English throne, now occupied by an old woman, must have seemed ripe for the taking if Essex should return from Ireland with victory laurels. He would virtually compel Elizabeth to marry him.

Shakespeare now wrote a propaganda play to rouse sentiment for Essex. The subject of the next chronicle was obvious: *Henry V.*

Prince Hal, the rowdy Prince depicted in *Henry IV*, would now become a resolute king. *Henry V* is the saga of England's most popular monarch, the beloved King Harry. As the Archbishop of Canterbury observes:

> The breath no sooner left his father's body,
> But that his wildness . . .
> Seemed to die too.

Canterbury marvels at the change.

> Never was such a sudden scholar made;
> Never came reformation in a flood.

He says of the young king's political ability:

> Turn him to any cause of policy,
> The Gordian knot of it he will unloose.

As a leader, Harry had developed character as well as charisma. He had "the art and practic part of life" that girded idealism with insight.

> Free from gross passion or of mirth or anger
> Constant in spirit, not swerving with the blood
> Not working with the eye without the ear
> And in purged judgment trusting neither.

King Harry was probably the ablest and most adored ruler in English history. Though Henry V led armies to win battles in France, he did not exploit that popularity with an abuse of power. Unlike other English kings, Henry V did not try to cow the courts or bypass Parliament.

The model Shakespeare used for the character of Henry V was arguably Essex. Through Southampton Shakespeare had come to know Essex, and the poet imagined him as a possible ruler, who would be like King Harry. (Overlooked in Shakespeare's portrait of Harry was the impetuous figure Essex had cut at court.)

Richard II had been an indirect attempt to shape political events, but *Henry V* was the first and only play in which Shakespeare inserted the politics of the day directly into the text of a play.

As actor as well as a playwright, Shakespeare himself would openly cheerlead the cause of Essex. England's greatest playwright had become a politician, openly advancing the fortunes of the would-be king.[1] Staging this play was almost like hosting a modern political fund-raiser. In a prologue to the fifth act, Shakespeare himself might have come on stage as a commentator and recited:

> How London doth pour out her citizens!
> The mayor and all his brethren in best sort,
> Like to the senators of the antique Rome,
> With the plebeians swarming at their heels,
> Go forth and fetch their conquering Caesar in:
> As, by a lower but high-loving, likelihood,
> Were now the general of our gracious empress,
> As in good time he may, from Ireland coming,
> Bringing rebellion broached on his sword,
> How many would the peaceful city quit,
> To welcome him!

In reality, however, Essex, though a courageous and charismatic figure, was no King Harry. He could be alternatively resolute and indecisive, generous and self-serving. Why would Shakespeare risk his career, if not his life, in open support of a move to seize the crown?

Historians rate Elizabeth I as one of the island's greatest monarchs. In her reign the Renaissance blossomed and commerce burgeoned. She succeeded her unloved sister Mary, who had tried to restore Catholicism and had married the King of Spain. Elizabeth had launched ships to explore the New World abroad, and at home she had kept Spain at bay. Why was Shakespeare not more admiring of Elizabeth? At least he might have appreciated her passion for the theater. After all, if Elizabeth had been a Puritan, or pious to the verge of penance, the chief glory of her reign, the drama, might never have quickened into life.

Shakespeare might have appreciated Elizabeth more if he had stayed in Stratford. But as an actor and playwright in London, he saw the aging Elizabeth and her court at too close a range. He observed all the vanities and petty power games played by her political advisers, like Cecil, Bacon, and Raleigh. They had, as Shakespeare later wrote in *Lear*, "the pate of a politician—one that could circumvent God." When Shakespeare backed Essex, he probably did so because the brave captain of arms represented something exciting and different. He had become disillusioned with the way the old Queen manipulated her court. In Essex, Shakespeare saw a leader who might rule as Henry V once had. Shakespeare liked Essex not so much for what he was, but what he might be.

Yet if defeated in Ireland, Essex never would head England. And unless more troops were dispatched to Ireland quickly, Essex would indeed be beaten. The stumbling block was Cecil, England's state treasurer and keeper of the royal purse, and the way to move Cecil was to rally public opinion. So Shakespeare wrote *Henry V* to shape public opinion.

Shakespeare saw in Elizabeth a ruler who was losing, along with her health and vitality, her hold on her subjects. The aging hand on the scepter was losing its grip. She was becoming too dependent on the palace guard and courtiers, whose agendas were tailored to their own ambitions. These court bureaucrats were the "caterpillars of the commonwealth," whom Shakespeare's Bolingbroke had vowed "to weed and pluck away" when he took the crown away from Richard II.

In *Henry V*, before the battle at Agincourt, Shakespeare has King Harry go in disguise and mingle with his troops to learn his subjects' unvarnished opinions of their king. Only a leader who is in contact with his people can inspire them.

Harry knows that a king cannot confuse his office with himself—that a crown alone cannot make character. A king is a man, and perforce, a lonely man.

> What infinite hearts-ease
> Must kings neglect, that private men enjoy!
> And what have kings that privates have not too,
> Save ceremony, save general ceremony.

Shakespeare's King Harry, like the real-life Churchill centuries later, knows how to tell his people what they were fighting and dying for. As Henry V, Richard Burbage would enjoy his greatest role since Richard III. English taverns rang with the poetry of the pep talks with which "King Harry" inspired his troops. The stirring words by Harry before the battle of Harfleur made the penny public forget about the fate of Falstaff, who has died in the first act.

> Once more unto the breach, dear friends once more;
> Or close the wall up with our English dead!
> In peace there's nothing so becomes a man
> As modest stillness and humility:
> But when the blast of war blows in our ears,
> Then imitate the action of the tiger,
> Stiffen the sinews, conjure up the blood.
>   . . .
> I see you stand like greyhounds in the slips,

Straining upon the start. The game's afoot:
Follow your spirit and upon this charge
Cry "God for Harry! England and Saint George!"

England once again had its nationalist pride rekindled. Ten years had passed since Philip II had launched the Spanish Armada, yet Spain still remained the "evil empire," in the words President Reagan used to describe the Soviets four centuries later. Now the wicked Spaniards were scheming to foment Irish rebellion—assisting the Irish chieftain Tyrone in his fight against the English. In such a time of patriotic fervor against Spain, Shakespeare's words became a popular litany, as George M. Cohan's "It's a Grand Old Flag" was in America in World War I and Irving Berlin's "God Bless America" in World War II. *Henry V* was a hit with Londoners.[2]

One of Winston Churchill's favorite films was the movie based on this Shakespearean drama, in which Sir Laurence Olivier, as King Harry, tells his men at Agincourt that their courage on St. Crispin's day would never be forgotten. Churchill's "finest hour" speech in 1940 owed much to Shakespeare.

This day is called the feast of Crispian;
He that outlives this day, and comes safe home,
Will stand a tip-toe when this day is named,
And rouse him at the name of Crispian.
He that shall live this day, and see old age,
Will yearly on the vigil feast his neighbors,
And say, "Tomorrow is Saint Crispian."

Richard Burton said that Churchill knew all the chronicles and tragedies by heart. Churchill, witnessed Burton, would sit in the first row and growl aloud in his inimitable voice all the lines of King Harry, Richard III, or Prince Hamlet. (Actors such as Burton did not always appreciate Churchill's unsolicited vocal contribution.)

King Harry's Crispian speech was also a favorite of John Kennedy, and the President's brother Robert often quoted the closing lines of the battle oration:

We few, we happy few, we band of brothers;
For he today that sheds his blood with me
Shall be my brother; be he ne'er so vile,
This day shall gentle his condition:
And gentlemen in England now a-bed
Shall think themselves accursed they were not here,

And hold their manholds cheap whiles any speaks
That fought with us upon Saint Crispin's day.

Certainly, Olivier brought a Camelot glow to his wartime film, playing
Henry V as another King Arthur in his rout of the corrupt and effete foe.
Today's movie audiences have the privilege of seeing Kenneth Branagh
give new dimension to the character of the young Plantagenet king.
Branagh, in his 1989 film, lets the viewer see the maturation of the
soldier-king from an unsure monarch to a steel tempered leader of men.
If Olivier dominated the screen, Branagh lets the English army share the
credit for the underdog victory at Agincourt. Under Branagh's direction,
the exhilaration and glamour of battle is stripped aside to reveal the mud
and blood.

In one significant way Shakespeare did not pattern Henry V after
Essex—the courtier was probably not a bumbling lover. Shakespeare in
his chronicle contrasts King Harry's warring and wooing. The blunt-talk-
ing soldier does not know how to court the French princess Katherine.

> Fair Katherine, and most fair,
> Will you vouchsafe to teach a soldier terms
> Such as will enter a lady's ear
> And plead his love-suit to her gentle heart?

The language barrier compounded Harry's problem. In the late 1590s
Shakespeare had moved in with the family of Christopher Mountjoy, a
maker of women's headdresses, whose most noted client was Queen
Elizabeth. The Mountjoys lived in Silver Street, a district of handsome
houses in the northwest of London. Mountjoy's daughter Mary, who
followed him in his trade, was being courted by Mountjoy's young
apprentice, Stephen Belott, a French Huguenot refugee.[3] Their language
difficulties inspired Shakespeare.

King: O fair Katherine! If you love me soundly with your French heart, I will
  be glad to hear you confess it brokenly with your English tongue. Do you
  like me, Kate?
Katharine: Pardonnez moi, I cannot tell vat is "like me."
King: An angel is like you, Kate, and you are like an angel.
Katharine: Que dit-il? que je suis semblable à les anges?

The passage, incidentally, is proof that Shakespeare understood French.
French would not have been difficult to learn, with his command of Latin,
and he could have practiced it with Belott in his Silver Street lodgings.

If at the close of the sixteenth century Henry V was viewed as the greatest leader in English history, the greatest ruler in all history was thought to be Julius Caesar. In Shakespeare's play of that name, he has a character describe him aptly: "Why, man, he doth bestride the narrow world/Like a Colossus."

It was not by happenstance that Shakespeare wrote *Julius Caesar* as soon as he had finished *Henry V*. In *Henry V* he wanted to rouse the English people, but in *Julius Caesar* he wanted to warn Essex. The tragic figure of Shakespeare's epic drama is Brutus, not Caesar.

Shakespeare began his play at the end of Plutarch's tale. Caesar, though now the emperor, is an old man who does not want younger ambitious men around him.

> Let me have men about me that are fat;
> Sleek-headed men, and such as sleep o' nights.
> Yond' Cassius has a lean and hungry look;
> He thinks too much: such men are dangerous.

Caesar did not trust such zealous aides, and he had reason. One of the slick assistants who had ingratiated himself into Caesar's inner circle was Decius.

When Cassius doubts that Caesar will come to the Capitol, Decius says he himself will persuade Caesar and then usher him to the assassination site. "Never fear that," says Decius. "If he be so resolved, I can o'ersway him." Decius then brags about how he has insinuated himself into Caesar's trust:

> When I tell him he hates flatterers,
> He says he does, being then most flattered.
> Let me work.

Nevertheless, it comes as no surprise to Caesar that Cassius and Decius are plotters—the shock is Brutus. Brutus is no palace functionary; he is a friend. Caesar sees in Brutus the nobility of ideals and honor.

For Shakespeare, Brutus might have been Essex and Caesar, the aging Elizabeth, whose rule grows more arbitrary with her age. "The abuse of greatness is when it disjoins/Remorse from power." Shakespeare foresees the danger of the charismatic dictator when he has Casca say:

> O, he sits high in all the people's hearts;
> And that which would appear offence in us

His countenance, like richest alchemy,
Will change to virtue and to worthiness.

Yet Shakespeare does not condone the greatest assassination in history ("O judgment, thou art fled to brutish beasts and men have lost their reason")—but he is warning that civil bloodshed is too great a price for power.

The plotters "cry out/Liberty, freedom and enfranchisement." Shakespeare, however, was no friend of the revolutionary, who in the name of ideals justifies his instruments of terror. He foresaw the Castros and the Khomeinis, whose resort to violence has led them to tyrannies worse than those they sought to overcome. After the stabbing of Caesar, Cassius congratulates his fellow conspirators:

How many ages hence
Shall this our lofty scene be acted over
In states unborn and accents yet unknown!

The play, however, is not about political violence, but political character. In bringing down the government of Rome, Brutus destroys himself. The "noble Brutus," has not the cynicism of a Cassius nor the guile of a Marc Antony. Ruthlessness and remorselessness were not the hallmarks of Brutus. Before the assassination he implores, "Let us be sacrificers, but not butchers."

Brutus was more introspective than an Essex. He could ponder the anatomy of assassination.

Between the acting of a dreadful thing
And the first motion, all the interim is
Like a phantasm or a hideous dream.

A Robespierre or a Lenin would not say, as Brutus did after the slaying, "not that I loved Caesar less, but that I loved Rome more. . . . As he was valiant, I honour him; as he was ambitious, I slew him." Nor would such a dictator give a forum to a potential rival of his own party, as Brutus did for Marc Antony.

Shakespeare, who would speech-write some of the greatest political orations in literature or history, would pen his most quoted of these in Antony's address. The speech structure is witness to Shakespeare's early classical schooling at King Edward VI's grammar school. It begins with an introduction, or what rhetoricians call the *proemium*, which is designed to gain the confidence of the audience:

> Friends, Romans, countrymen, lend me your ears;
> I come to bury Caesar, not to praise him.
> The evil that men do lives after them;
> The good is oft interred with their bones;
> So let it be with Caesar.

A great speaker does not persuade a skeptical audience by trying to overpower it at the start. So Antony masks his passion, allowing only a hint of sardonic edge when he praises Brutus:

> For Brutus is an honourable man;
> So are they all, all honourable men.

The proemium is followed by the *narratio*, which is the building of the case. For Antony the case is the charge of ambition, leveled against Caesar by Brutus and his followers. Antony turns Brutus's label "ambitious" to Caesar's advantage:

> When that the poor have cried, Caesar has wept:
> Ambition should be made of sterner stuff.

Antony then offers a litany of Caesar's good works to the Roman people, capping it with:

> O judgment! thou art fled to brutish beasts,
> And men have lost their reason.

In classical rhetoric the narratio, or gist of the argument, is followed by the *proof* which is the message the argument proves, like the Q.E.D. (*quod erat demonstrandum*) in geometry. After reading a speech draft I once prepared for him, President Eisenhower once demanded, "What's the Q.E.D.? What is it you want the audience to do? If you don't know what the bottom-line message is, you're wasting my time." Antony's "proof" is that the real loser in the killing is not Caesar, but the people.

> Great Caesar fell.
> O what a fall was there, my countrymen!
> Then I, and you, and all of us fell down,
> Whilst bloody treason flourish'd over us.

Antony would contrast the actions of the conspirators with the deeds of Caesar in the final stage of the classical speech structure, which was the *epilogue*, or what today is called the peroration. In musical terms this would be the coda.

Antony wins the attention of the audience at the beginning, then builds his logical case for action. The epilogue or coda is the call to arms. Though Antony masks his appeal with modesty, it is nevertheless a call for mob revolt. It is the backhandedness that makes it brilliant.

> I come not, friends, to steal away your hearts:
> I am no orator, as Brutus is;
> But, as you know me all, a plain blunt man,
> . . .
> For I have neither wit, nor words, nor worth,
> Action, nor utterance, nor the power of speech,
> To stir men's blood: I only speak right on.
> . . .
> Put a tongue
> In every wound of Caesar, that should move
> The stones of Rome to rise and mutiny.

Antony's speech is a study of the persuasive technique to use with a potentially hostile audience. Shakespeare, as an actor, understood the audience, and as a student he had read the great orations in Cicero and Plutarch. The result, though fictional, was literature's greatest speech. Antony's speech sets the stage for a civil war, which slowly tears at Brutus's soul until he is driven to take his own life.

Although *Julius Caesar* was almost as popular as *Henry V*, its production was suddenly cancelled. At the same time that Tyrone's forces were closing in on Essex in Ireland, Burbage's Theatre had to shut down in London.

NOTES

1. Clara Longworth de Chambrun, *Shakespeare: A Portrait Restored* (London: Holis & Carter, 1957), p. 217; Peter Quennell, *Shakespeare: The Poet and His Background* (Cleveland: World, 1963), p. 222.

2. Ibid., p. 213.

3. Marquette Shute, *Shakespeare of London* (New York: Dutton, 1949), p. 277.

CHAPTER FOURTEEN

Eviction and Erection

To business that we love we rise betime.

Antony and Cleopatra
act 4, scene 4

From the beginning, James Burbage's success in giving Londoners their first theater had exceeded his expectations. In the 1590s he and his son Cuthbert, who had taken over the task of business manager, had raked in receipts at their Shoreditch playhouse. The Chronicles, which their actor Will Shakespeare had adapted and scripted from the pages of Holinshed, had struck a popular chord with London audiences, and these Shakespeare plays had helped make the theater a commercial triumph.

The Burbage troupe had also pioneered a more lifelike acting style. This naturalism, which was in contrast with the more grandiloquent histrionics of the day, became recognized as the hallmark of the company. This professionalism, along with the Shakespeare genius for adapting old plots, propelled the Burbage company to the forefront.[1]

Indeed, as we have seen, the lord chamberlain, Lord Hunsdon, a cousin of the Queen (son of Mary, the sister of Anne Boleyn) had adopted the Burbage company. They now called themselves the Lord Chamberlain's Men. The new name attested to the rising prominence of the Theatre and its popularity with playgoers.[2] The Theatre, as Shakespeare said about Julius Caesar, now bestrode "the [acting] world like a colossus."

Yet, like Caesar, it would be brought down and destroyed. Giles Allen, the owner of the Shoreditch land upon which the Theatre had been built, was jealous of the Burbage family success. As the Burbages' lease neared expiration, Allen jacked up the terms for renegotiation. The exorbitant raise in rent forced James Burbage to look elsewhere.

Burbage was not a young man. In his late middle age, he suddenly saw a threat to all that he had built in his lifetime. Instead of yielding to Allen's extortionate demands, however, he gambled on even a bigger dream. He decided to buy an old disused theater in the Blackfriars locality of London. This area was both a liberty and an exclusively residential section. In other words, it represented the best of both worlds, being free from City Council regulations and also free of the riff-raff that lived around Shoreditch.[3]

Burbage had the idea of converting this auditorium, which had often been used for private showings to the rich families of Blackfriars. At Christmas time, for example, the choir school at St. Paul's Cathedral would stage skits for the amusement of the neighborhood gentry. For a one-time carpenter from Warwickshire, this modern, all-season theater right in the middle of London's most exclusive environs was the ultimate dream. Burbage put down his life's savings to convert the old stage hall into the first roofed and heated theater for the elite of London. Blackfriars was a community of about five acres, inhabited by nobles and gentlemen. It had a special porter to shut the four gates leading into the residential enclave. Burbage and his family had at last arrived.

But the same lords who regularly attended Burbage's Theatre in Shoreditch did not want a theater bordering their private residences. To them it was the equivalent of having pornographic movies just off Park Avenue, New York, or burlesque shows in Belgravia, London. Even Lord Hunsdon, who was the patron of Burbage's acting company, signed a petition to the Privy Council protesting any performances. The Privy Council, some of whom, like Hunsdon, lived in Blackfriars, still prohibited the staging of public performances. A few months later, in January 1597, James Burbage, who had tied up a great deal of money in the Blackfriars' venture, would die a broken man.[4]

His son Cuthbert was then forced to reopen negotiations with Allen. The company's lease would expire in January 1599. Finally, in the fall of 1598, Cuthbert agreed to the exorbitant rent of £24 a year. The old rent had been £14.[5] But just before Christmas, Allen reneged. It was clear that Allen wanted not more rent but the Theatre itself.

The Burbage family was outraged. Why should they allow another company to stage plays in the theater they had founded? It was their company that had built the reputation of the Theatre. It was their plays, the best of which Shakespeare had written, that had brought the Theatre fame and success.

The Burbages were not going to let another promoter cash in on their investment. But what could they do? They would be evicted from their theater home, and they lacked the money to buy a new one. Most of their capital had been spent in refurbishing the ill-fated Blackfriars. So the Burbage family turned to the members of the company, who pooled their resources and secretly bought a new site across London Bridge on the west side of the Thames River embankment. Then, when Allen was away in his country house at Christmas time, they mobilized a posse of players and set workers to tear down the Theatre. Down it came, timber by timber, section by section, in order, each carefully numbered, marked, and stacked for reassembling. Then they carted the numbered parts down the Shoreditch and Bishopsgate Roads to the Thames, where they ferried them to the south embankment and constructed a new theater out of the timber of the old one.[6]

The new site was right next to a popular London attraction, the Bear Garden, which featured fights between mastiff bulldogs and Russian bears. Shakespeare mentions the most famous bear, Sackerson, in both *Henry V* and *Merry Wives of Windsor.* In the latter Slender says:

I have seen Sackerson loose twenty times, and have taken him by the chain; but I warrant you, the women have so cried and shrieked at it that it passed.

The new theater that Cuthbert Burbage built was called the Globe, and a huge orb was hung alongside it to illustrate the name. Actually, the orb, or globe, was held by Hercules, with the motto, *Totus Mundus Agit Histrionem*, which might be loosely translated as "All the world's a stage." The name Globe invites a double interpretation, since it suggested the theater's quasi-circular shape and also connotes the adventurous age that Elizabethans were experiencing, with their travels and explorations.

The new theater was the same as the original, except that it was polygonal in shape. Otherwise, there was the same jutting stage, with boxes in front for the lords and behind them the open pits for the penny public.[7]

Just as the Globe had a shape that was new, so the Burbage company was also reorganized. Shakespeare was a one-tenth partner (one of five sharers in one part) in the new theater, and in the new company.[8] As the stucco and timbered Globe rose to completion, Shakespeare might have reflected on the reputation he had built in the 12 years he had been in London.

When Edmund Spenser, the author of *The Faerie Queene*, died in 1599, Shakespeare, as England's greatest poet, was a pallbearer, as the poet's coffin was borne to its niche in Westminster Abbey. Shakespeare was chosen despite the fact he was still an actor performing on stage. To have a theatrical performer featured in the Abbey was close to sacrilege. Shakespeare went there with his Warwickshire childhood friend and poet, Michael Drayton. In addition, Ben Jonson, John Marston, and George Chapman, who was famous for his poetic translation of Homer, also took part in the Abbey services. This honor extended to Shakespeare gives the lie to those who argue that Shakespeare was actually neither poet nor playwright.[9]

Starting as a prompter, on the lowest rung of a dubious profession, Shakespeare had become the most successful playwright of his time. The profits from his plays had bought him a splendid country house in Stratford. His fame, as well as the prominence he had achieved as a poet, had won for him the coat of arms his family had long sought. He was the first actor to be a gentleman, and he was also the first actor to be active in the politics of his day. Yet if Shakespeare was fascinated by the exercise of power, he was also repelled by the self-serving ambitions and hollow vanities of London court life.

NOTES

1. S. H. Burton, *Shakespeare's Life and Stage* (Edinburgh: W. & R. Chambers, 1989), p. 189.

2. Peter Levi, *The Life and Times of William Shakespeare* (New York: Holt, 1988), p. 147; Joseph Quincy Adams, *A Life of William Shakespeare* (Boston: Houghton Mifflin, 1923), pp. 188–90.

3. Marquette Shute, *Shakespeare of London* (New York: Dutton, 1949), pp. 206–9.

4. Ibid.

5. Levi, *Life and Times of Shakespeare*, p. 190.

6. Shute, *Shakespeare of London*, pp. 210–11; Burton, *Shakespeare's Life and Stage*, p. 97.

7. Peter Quennell, *Shakespeare: The Poet and His Background* (Cleveland: World, 1963), pp. 154–56; Shute, *Shakespeare of London*, pp. 212–13.

8. Levi, *Life and Times of Shakespeare*, p. 190; Shute, *Shakespeare of London*, pp. 209–10.

9. Clara Longworth de Chambrun, *Shakespeare: A Portrait Restored* (London: Holis & Carter, 1957), pp. 221–22.

CHAPTER FIFTEEN

The Deer and the Bear

But bear-like, I must fight the course

Macbeth
act 5, scene 7

Like Washington, D.C., at the present time, London at the turn of the sixteenth century had developed a social and cultural life that fed on political power. London was the place for all the fun high society knew how to have—court dances and tournaments, where courtiers and ladies flaunted their silks and jewels. The Court was the arena in which the imperious Queen manipulated her ambitious courtiers. Political intrigues and maneuverings for power dominated people's lives. In the corridors of the White House today, no less than the Whitehall of Elizabethan days, we "hear poor rogues talk of court news and we'll talk with them too, who loses and who wins; who's in, who's out."

Yet what Shakespeare heard and saw at Court must have made him yearn for the holidays. Shakespeare had become a squire, as his mother's father Robert Arden once had been.[1] He had redeemed his own father's failure. His visits to Stratford were now more frequent. He had to look after the huge house he had recently bought and was now renting to his childhood friend Thomas Greene, a lawyer.[2]

After all, Will regarded himself as a squire of Stratford, even though he spent most of his life in London. Like Mark Twain, who spent most of his life in the East writing about his youth on the Mississippi, Shakespeare romanticized the Stratford village life he had left. The country, with its town fairs and village dances, seemed a merrier place. Stratford was a community where every shopkeeper, like his father, was known and every occupation seemed personified—the pedlar, the tinker, the blacksmith. The bright texture of country life, as well as the superstitious country beliefs in magical spirits and elves, fed the playwright's imagination.

In his early comedy *Love's Labour's Lost*, Shakespeare ended with a picture of Warwickshire in winter that reminds one of a Robert Frost poem about New England:

> When icicles hang by the wall,
>   And Dick the shepherd blows his nail,
> And Tom bears logs into the hall,
>   And milk comes frozen home in pail
>   . . .
>   And coughing drowns the parson's saw,
> And birds set brooding in the snow,
>   And Marian's nose looks red and raw,
> When roasted crabs hiss in the bowl,
> Then nightly sings the staring owl,
>   Tu-whit;
> Tu-who, A merry note,
> While greasy Joan doth keel the pot.

In London another playwright arose to challenge Shakespeare's dominance. The challenger was Ben Jonson, eight years his junior. Both had started their theatrical careers as actors, but there the similarity ended. Shakespeare was fair and sunny, while Jonson was dark and heavy set. If in grace and gentleness Shakespeare was a deer, Jonson in his hulking, bellowing presence was a bear.[3] One might say Jonson was almost Falstaffian in appearance and demeanor—except that Jonson had talent to back up his bravado.

In London's Mermaid Tavern on Broad Street, Jonson liked to pontificate to his fellow playwrights, including Shakespeare. The tavern, hosted by Shakespeare's friend William Johnson, was a meeting place where, besides the wine, theories on literature and politics were imbibed and savored.

There, on the first Friday of the month, in a tradition started by Sir Walter Raleigh, noblemen and lawyers, playwrights and actors met to discuss their cases and their roles in the arts.[4] Shakespeare may have described the Mermaid, in *Taming of the Shrew*:

> Do as adversaries do in law
> Strive mightily but eat and drink as friends.

Thomas Fuller wrote in his *Worthies of England* (1662) that Shakespeare enjoyed those drinking sessions. "His genius was generally jocular, inclining him to festivity." Yet Shakespeare's love of fellowship did not include drunken sprees. Christopher Beeston told John Aubrey that Shakespeare "wouldn't be debauched." A sociable drink or two at the Mermaid was one thing, but Shakespeare stayed away from the sort of "heavy-headed revel" he would later describe in *Hamlet*.

Some writers, like attorneys, love argument for the sake of argument. Shakespeare was not one of those; he preferred the role of observer to that of advocate. Yet Shakespeare had his likes and dislikes—opinions reflected in his plays that may also have figured in his conversation. In government he had contempt for pompous justices (*Merry Wives of Windsor*), officious administrators (*Hamlet* and *Measure for Measure*), and lying politicians (*King Lear*). Even worse than the politicians were the parasites at Court—particularly the scented and effeminate men, like Hotspur's courtier and Osric in *Hamlet*. Of course, in the theater he would have expressed his distaste for histrionic actors and ad-libbing clowns (*Hamlet*).

If Shakespeare enjoyed the fellowship of writers, Ben Jonson relished the fights that were ignited by the clash of authors' convictions. In the seventeenth century Bishop Thomas Fuller would write in his *Worthies of England* that Jonson found Shakespeare an elusive foe.

Jonson, according to Fuller's account, was like "a Spanish great galleon, . . . built for higher learning, solid, but slow in his performance," but Shakespeare was a swifter, smaller English frigate, "lesser in bulk but lighter in sailing and could turn with all tides, tack about and take advantage of all winds by the quickness of his wit and invention."[5] In his tavern chair, Jonson would roar out his sacred classical tenets and rake over the works of those who violated them.

Sometimes Shakespeare was the target of his jibes. To Jonson, Shakespeare's chronicles had not really been plays, and Shakespeare wasn't really a dramatist. A true dramatist would not flout the unities by mixing comedy and tragedy in the same drama. A real playwright, bellowed Jonson, cannot violate the literary laws, which the Greeks developed and the Romans adopted. Neither *King John* nor *Richard II*, for example, presented a heroic character with an innate and tragic flaw.[6]

When told that the fast-writing Shakespeare never blotted a script page with an error, Jonson expostulated, "Would that he had blotted a thousand pages!" Jonson thought a true scholar would have many "blots," or crossed-out passages, corrected by research and revision.

When Shakespeare arrived in London in 1586, Jonson was studying the classics there, at the prestigious Westminister School. Jonson's hopes of continuing his classical education at Oxford crumbled when the death of his father forced him to take up bricklaying, the occupation of his new stepfather. Laying bricks was many a social step down from the profession of teaching and preaching his deceased father had once pursued.[7]

Like Shakespeare, Jonson had chosen the stage as his ladder to success. He became an actor, but he was not a particularly good one. A fellow actor panned a performance of his, saying he had "laid a brick" as an actor. ("Lay a brick" is the English equivalent of the American "lay an egg".) The hot-headed Jonson challenged the actor to a duel. The foe arrived at the appointed place and hour, with a sword longer than Jonson's. Jonson could have honorably refused combat, but he braved it out and stabbed his opponent through the heart.[8]

For the killing Jonson was sentenced to death, but he escaped execution by claiming the ancient right of clergy—those learned in the Latin Bible could save themselves from execution by proving they could parse and translate a Biblical verse. Jonson asked to be showed the first verse of the 21st Psalm (nicknamed the "neck verse"), and he easily read it. Nevertheless, his property was confiscated and he was carted off to Tyburn prison, where Jonson had the capital "T" of Tyburn prison branded on his thumb as the felon's mark of his jail record.

When Jonson left prison, his head was full of ideas for plays. One of these was *Every Man in His Humour*, which he tried in vain to get a company to stage. In those days a playwright with a new script, according to Joseph Papp, would call on a company right after a performance. While relaxing with tankards of ale, the half-dressed actors would listen to the playwright read his new play.

But the various companies would not even let Jonson inside the door. After all, the theatrical community no doubt saw Jonson as one who killed one of the fraternity, and his arrogant pretentiousness made them slow to forget it. Jonson then turned to the "king of the theater," Shakespeare, whose plays he had so gratuitously condemned. Shakespeare read *Every Man in His Humour* and persuaded the Lord Chamberlain's Men to stage it. Jonson was so grateful that he listed the name of William Shakespeare above that of Richard Burbage in the playbill of the comedy, in which both performed.[9]

The play was a hit and introduced a new kind of comedy to the Elizabethan stage. If Marlowe yearned to be an English Aeschylus of tragedy, Jonson wanted to be the English Aristophanes of comedy. Jonson put a different twist on the word "humour" in the title of the play and made it the comic version of a tragic flaw. In Jonson's comedies the main character always has an idiosyncracy or foible that determines his downfall.

For a while Jonson was the rage. The young playwright followed his success with a sequel, *Every Man Out of His Humour*.[10] Some playwrights might have found it difficult to adapt to the tastes whetted by the Jonson plays, but not Shakespeare. He could move from tragedy to comedy as easily as George Gershwin could shift from "Rhapsody in Blue" to a musical such as *Boy Crazy*. If Shakespeare could chronicle history as Robert Sherwood did in *Abe Lincoln in Illinois*, he could also be like Thornton Wilder, with ideas for farce and comedy.

Shakespeare would soon make the classics-loving Jonson yesterday's news, however. A revue performed at Cambridge University featured Richard Burbage and Will Kempe, who had come to the University to recruit students for their company. Kempe, in the skit, said:

Few of the university pen plays well. They smell too much of that writer Ovid and talk too much of Proserpina and Jupiter. Why here's our fellow Shakespeare puts them all down—ay and Ben Jonson too! O that Ben Jonson is a pestilent fellow: he brought up Horace giving the poets a pill, but our fellow Shakespeare has given him a purge.[11]

Jonson stands in marked contrast to the older Shakespeare. First, in acting, Jonson was boisterous, and his ranting made him a ham. Shakespeare, in contrast, was more understated. The explosive energy of Jonson did not stand up to the gallant grace of Shakespeare.

Furthermore, Jonson, unlike Shakespeare, had no respect for women. Not one of his plays featured an attractive woman. Shakespeare, however, was the first English playwright to portray women with depth.

Unlike his contemporary dramatists, Shakespeare assigned a predominate place to women and to love. He endows his heroines with the gifts of personality and intelligence. They are generous, courageous, loyal, and inflexible on questions of honor. Shakespeare saw a beloved woman not as a toy but as the goddess of the hearth. If Jonson saw women as weak and fickle, Shakespeare viewed them as strong and fearless in defense of their honor and their home.

Shakespeare was popular in the theater world. If Jonson had few friends, he had his devotees, whom he affectionately called "Ben's tribe." Yet he also had a legion of enemies.

Shakespeare tolerated the antics of Jonson with bemused affection. He once sent to Jonson, on the baptism of his godson, a "Latin spoon." A Latin spoon was made of pewter. The gift was a playful gibe at Jonson, who slavishly translated and adapted Roman plays, like *Sejanus*, into English. The thrust was that Jonson could then, with his Latin alchemy, translate the pewter spoon into gold. Jonson, despite his literary disagreements with Shakespeare, loved him for both his gentleness and his generosity of spirit.

The enchantment that marked the character of Shakespeare would suffuse his comedies. His comic touch would soon light up the London stage.

NOTES

1. Joseph Quincy Adams, *A Life of William Shakespeare* (Boston: Houghton Mifflin, 1923), p. 256.

2. Ibid., p. 255.

3. Ibid., p. 242.

4. Ibid., pp. 241–42.

5. Thomas Fuller, *Worthies of England*, 2 vols. (London: J. G., W. L., & W. G., 1662). In 1660 Fuller collected material in a short encyclopaedia arranged by county. The biographical material about Shakespeare was found under "Warwickshire."

6. Marquette Shute, *Shakespeare of London* (New York: Dutton, 1949), pp.202–4, 270–71; Peter Quennell, *Shakespeare: The Poet and His Background* (Cleveland: World, 1963), pp. 193–96.

7. Ibid., pp. 190–94.

8. Shute, *Shakespeare of London*, pp. 202–4.

9. Quennell, *Shakespeare*, pp. 90–91; Adams, *A Life of Shakespeare*, pp. 272–74, 276–77.

10. Adams, *Life of Shakespeare*, pp. 274–77; Quennell, *Shakespeare*, p. 188.

11. Quoted in *The Return from Parnassus, Part II*, ed. Tucker Brooke (New York: AMS Press, 1912), p. 38.

CHAPTER SIXTEEN

Romantic Entanglements

If thou remembered'st not the slightest folly
That ever love did make thee run into
Thou hast not loved.

As You Like It
act 2, scene 4

The popularity of Jonson's comedies now spurred Shakespeare's pen, and in short order he scribbled out a trilogy of comedies. These are among his most affectionately regarded: *Much Ado About Nothing*, *As You Like It*, and what he titled *What You Will*.[1]

The blithe titles suggest not only the spirit of the three plays but the quick and easy style of the writing.[2] Perhaps the titles also suggest the buoyancy and well-being of Shakespeare's life at the time. London's greatest poet and playwright was now relishing another life as a newly minted country squire. In *As You Like It*, Shakespeare has the Duke say:

Hath not old custom made this life more sweet
Than that of painted pomp?

Some might expect Shakespeare to be romantic in the manner of Keats, Byron, or Wordsworth, but he would be better compared to Sir Walter Scott, who transformed old Scottish tales into historical novels and converted his storytelling talent into profit to build his castle at Abbotsford. The plays Shakespeare wrote were set in Italy or France, but they were shaped by the country and peopled by the country folk he knew at Stratford.

All three plays involve romances that become entangled by farcical misadventures before the lovers end up in each other's arms. The devices for complication include cross-dressing (*As You Like It*), a misinterpreted letter (*What You Will*), and banishment (*As You Like It*).

The heroines of the plays, Beatrice, Rosalind, and Viola, are delightful concoctions. George Bernard Shaw said that Rosalind in *As You Like It* was "to the actress what Hamlet is to the actor." Shaw rhapsodized about this daughter of the banished Duke as "an extension into five acts of the most affectionate, fortunate, delightful five minutes in the life of a charming woman."[3]

Shakespeare had adapted the character from a popular prose romance entitled *Rosalynd*. The author, Thomas Lodge, had written the love tale after returning from the Canary Islands in the 1580s.[4]

Interestingly, the story has been passed down that the person who played Rosalind when it was staged at the Globe may have been none other than Shakespeare's little brother Edmond, who had left Stratford to follow in the footsteps of his famous brother, although many scholars think it would have been too important a role for the neophyte Edmond. Edmond was sixteen years younger than the playwright—only two years senior to his niece Susanna, Will Shakespeare's eldest. Unlike Will, Edmond probably had the boyish face and smallish figure needed to take on women's parts. (Edmond was not the only one of the Shakespeare clan to seek the stage in imitation of their famous relative. William Hart, the son of William's sister Joan, would join his uncle's old company in 1607.[5])

If Edmond needed help in this challenging role as Rosalind,[6] the help was right on stage. Adam, the old man, was played by his older brother.[7] Sixty years later, someone who remembered enjoying *As You Like It* in his youth spoke of having seen [Shakespeare] . . . impersonate a decrepit old man.

[He] wore a long beard and appeared so weak and drooping and unable to walk that he was forced to be supported and carried by another person to a table at which he was seated among some other company and one of them sung a song.[8]

Shakespeare's personal beliefs are reflected most in the character of Jaques. Monsieur Jaques is the play's philosopher ("All the world's a stage . . ."). Jaques is described:

> He pierceth through
> The body of the country, city court
> Yea, and of this life

At another point Shakespeare expressed through Jaques the result of his own observations:

I have neither the scholar's melancholy which is emulation; nor the musician's which is fantastical; nor the courtier's which is proud; nor the soldier's which is ambitious; nor the lawyer's which is politic; nor the lady's which is nice; nor the lover's which is all of these; but it is a melancholy of mine own, compounded of many samples extracted from many objects; and indeed, the sundry contemplation of my travels, in which my often rumination wraps me in a most humorous sadness.

Jaques, who once saw through the intrigues of a court, now peers beneath the simplicities of forest life.

In his middle thirties, as actor, director, and playwright, Shakespeare was no doubt enjoying himself. England's most famous man of the theater inserts himself at will in these plays. He plants Arden, the beloved woods of his Warwickshire youth, in a medieval duchy of France, where the action of *As You Like It* takes place. The trees of the real Forest of Arden supplied the timbers for the roof beams and wall posts of Stratford's houses. The olive trees, as well as the lion, in the *As You Like It* Arden came from Shakespeare's imagination. Shakespeare then crafts a deft allusion to his late mentor and friend Christopher Marlowe, affectionately calling him "dear shepherd."

> Dear shepherd, now I find thy saw of might
> Who ever loved that loved not at first sight.

The quoted line was from Marlowe's *Hero and Leander*.

As Shakespeare paid a tribute to the playwright who preceded him, in *What You Will* he would also acknowledge the one who would follow him—Ben Jonson. Of all his plays, this one has the most titles. Shakespeare published it as *What You Will*, but today most know it by the irrelevant title, *Twelfth Night*. It was rechristened that when played in Whitehall, at the Christmas-season celebration.

But in Shakespeare's time the play had still a third title. The actors and playbills called *What You Will* by the name of the Puritan whose priggish ways would insure his downfall—*Malvolio*.[9] In a sense, that built-in comeuppance is the sort of "humor" that Ben Jonson might have incorporated into one of his own leading characters.

Next to Falstaff, Malvolio was the favorite character of the penny public. If they laughed *with* Falstaff, they laughed at Malvolio. He is a lonely figure; like the Jew Shylock, the Puritan Malvolio is not accepted in the community. By his own reckoning an upright man of worth, Malvolio is not surprised that a pretty young woman such as Olivia should have designs on him. So when he thinks he is receiving a note encouraging his affections, he is misled. The letter is deceptive.

The number of Puritans making plays was proportionately as small as the number of "born-again" producers, directors, or actors in the movie and television industries today. The penny public, no less than the players, found the smug, middle-class pretentiousness of the Puritans tedious. Sir Toby Belch, who makes Malvolio his target, is an aristocratic Falstaff. (Prince Hal's roistering knight had only earned his "Sir" by taking the ignominious route of forcing drunks and delinquents into military service). Belch is the younger son, the professionless gentleman who hunts and shoots and trades locker-room stories. He shamelessly lives off his relatives, plus a little by his wits. His type can still be found in London clubs, and his American equivalent is a Faulkner "good ole boy" of patrician family in today's South. He is a bit of a bully, as well as a boozer. The play's most quoted line is in the scene when Sir Toby challenges Malvolio, where he needles the old Puritan. "Dost thou think, because thou art virtuous, there shall be no more cakes and ale?"

Some scholars speculate that Shakespeare's father had partially inspired the bibulous Sir Toby, as well as Falstaff. John Shakespeare was a jolly soul, whose taste for the tankard continued long after he was promoted from his first municipal job as an ale taster.[10]

The puritanical Malvolio may have been modeled from life. His original was Sir Thomas Hoby, a spindle-shanked and hunch-backed little man who had made himself a well known figure of ridicule in a lawsuit. It seems that once, while at his home in Yorkshire, Sir Thomas had tried to suppress the Christmas merrymaking of some Catholic neighbors. A few days later the neighbors entered his home in Hoby's absence and helped themselves to his cakes and ale. The offended Hoby took the trivial matter to court.

"Sir Thomas Hoby" sounds like "Sir Toby." The chime of name and transference of character from Malvolio to Sir Toby is a typical twist of Shakespeare's inventive mind. Yet Shakespeare's borrowing of Sir Thomas Hoby may have been political as well as playful; it was a prediction of the Cromwellian zeal.

Will Kempe played neither Sir Toby nor Malvolio. The role that would be his most remembered in this trilogy of comedies was that of Dogberry, the bumbling policeman in *Much Ado About Nothing*. This pompous constabulary "ass" struck a chord with Elizabethans.

When he apprehends what turns out to be the wrong man, Dogberry reports to Leonato, the governor,

One word, Sir! Our watch, sir, have indeed comprehended [sic] two aspicious [sic] persons, and we would have them this morning examined before your worship.

The officious and rotund Dogberry foreshadows a combination of Dickens's Mr. Bumble and Sheridan's Mrs. Malaprop. To Dogberry falls that most misquoted line, "Comparisons are odorous." He was not untypical of the Elizabethan lower classes, with their awkward attempts at self-improvement.

Dogberry was the last great role for Will Kempe. He retired giving his share in the Globe Theatre to his friend, Shakespeare, and shortly thereafter, in 1598, Kempe announced his intention to dance from London to Norwich. In 1600 he would "jig" the 48 miles, greeted at each town along the way with cakes, pies, and ale, served by legions of his admirers. He followed this triumph with a tale of his trek, entitled "The Ninth Wonder of the World."[11]

Perhaps the Burbage company was not entirely unhappy with the departure of its leading clown. Kempe was a scene stealer, whose outrageous antics were sometimes resented by his acting colleagues and thought unprofessional. Kempe made an art of playing the fool, but he was shrewd enough to know how to market himself. As a man of little education, he had none of the artistic graces of Richard Burbage, who was a painter, or of a Shakespeare, who was a poet. Yet his quick wit and talent for improvisation make it clear that his clownishness masked a high intelligence.

The model for Dogberry, whom Kempe played, was found in a constable Shakespeare had encountered in Long Grendon, Oxfordshire,[12] a town along the route north from Oxford to Stratford. And while Shakespeare was writing these comic romantic mix-ups, he may also have been weaving an entanglement of his own, having to do with his journeying back and forth from London to Stratford.

At Oxford, which was a half-way point, Shakespeare used to stop for lodging at the Crown Inn. The tavern owner was Robert Davenant, who is described by the Oxford historian Anthony a'Wood as "an admirer and lover of plays," although "he was never seen to laugh." His young wife, on the other hand, is pictured as "a very beautiful woman and of very good wit and of conversation extremely agreeable."[13] The vivacious Jane Davenant was in contrast not only to her dour husband but to Shakespeare's Puritan wife. Shakespeare would have been less than human if he did not find it delightful to spend hours in the company of this brunette beauty who, unlike his wife, loved the theater and was enchanted by theatrical luminaries.

The second child of the Davenants was named William Davenant, and Shakespeare was made his godfather. A half-century later Davenant would restyle his surname fashionably as D'Avenant, when he was appointed Poet Laureate of England. One wit at the time said he should have spelled it "*D'Avon* ant."[14]

William d'Avenant might have gained from the association with his godfather his taste for the theater, but from whom did he inherit his talent? We do not know for sure whether the Restoration playwright was the son of a bar owner or the son of the Bard. But d'Avenant himself would boast that Shakespeare was his sire, even though the claim stained the reputation of his mother.

Four facts survive about the relationship between William Shakespeare and William d'Avenant. First, of course, d'Avenant was the acknowledged namesake and godson of the playwright. Second, young D'Avenant at the age of 11 wrote a tender "Ode in the Remembrance of William Shakespeare." Third, Aubrey reported that Shakespeare once "showered" a hundred kisses on his godson. Fourth, the poet Dryden reported that d'Avenant had in his house the Chandos portrait of Shakespeare, which Dryden claimed had been painted by Richard Burbage.[15] (Dryden himself ordered a copy of the Burbage portrait from a celebrated court painter of the day.) Finally, it is said Shakespeare gave a valued letter from King James as a gift to his godson.[16]

NOTES

1. Marquette Shute, *Shakespeare of London* (New York: Dutton, 1949), p. 216; Tucker Brooke, *Shakespeare of Stratford* (New Haven, Conn.: Yale University Press, 1926), p. 119.

2. Joseph Quincy Adams, *A Life of William Shakespeare* (Boston: Houghton Mifflin, 1923), p. 292. "His retention of the older title *What You Will*, however, serves to reveal the essential kinship of the play with the two other members of the trilogy."

3. George Bernard Shaw, *Shaw on Shakespeare*, ed. Edwin Wilson (Salem, N.H.: Ayer, 1961).

4. Shute, *Shakespeare of London*, p. 216.

5. S. H. Burton, *Shakespeare's Life and Stage* (Edinburgh: W. & R. Chambers, 1989), p. 157.

6. Clara Longworth de Chambrun, *Shakespeare: A Portrait Restored* (London: Holis & Carter, 1957), p. 131.

7. Peter Quennell, *Shakespeare: The Poet and His Background* (Cleveland: World, 1963), p. 185.

8. Adams, *Life of Shakespeare*, pp. 290–91.

9. Adams, *Life of Shakespeare*, p. 292; Shute, *Shakespeare of London*, p. 216.

10. Clara Longworth de Chambrun, *Shakespeare: Actor-Poet* (London: Appleton, 1927), p. 5.

11. Quennell, *Shakespeare*, p. 187; *Adams, Life of Shakespeare*, p. 329.

12. Quennell, *Shakespeare*, p. 182.

13. Anthony a'Wood, quoted in Adams, *Life of Shakespeare*, p. 389.

14. Chambrun, *Shakespeare: Actor-Poet*, p. 162.

15. Ibid., p. 161.

It was D'Avenant, son of the hostess of that inn (the Crown), who possessed the best contemporary portrait of Shakespeare. Dryden says this "Chandos" canvas [named for the Duke of Chandos, who later acquired it] was painted by Burbage, that Betterton [an actor] obtained it from D'Avenant, and that Dryden himself obtained a copy from the original by the celebrated court painter, Sir Godfrey Knellor.

16. Adams, *Life of Shakespeare*, pp. 389–92; Quennell, *Shakespeare*, pp. 294–95. Shute, *Shakespeare of London*, pp. 349–51, questions the reliability of D'Avenant. "D'Avenant was not above reinforcing his claims as a writer by hinting broadly that he was actually Shakespeare's son."

CHAPTER SEVENTEEN

Rebellion and Revival

By the Lord, our plot is a good plot as ever was laid; our friends true
and constant: a good plot, good friends, and full of expectation.

I Henry IV
act 2, scene 3

While Shakespeare was sampling the pleasures of squiredom in Stratford,
his patron Southampton was in Ireland, pinned down with Essex by the
forces of Irish rebellion. Cecil had reneged on a promise to aid Essex.

Yet Essex, who faced certain defeat on a foreign shore, managed to save
his army. Unlike the English at Dunkirk four centuries later, Essex somehow managed to wangle from the Irish chieftain, Tyrone, terms for safe
withdrawal.[1] It was a survival that had the color of success.

This was not quite the scenario Cecil, Elizabeth's chief minister in
Whitehall, had devised for Essex. Perhaps Essex was not coming back to
London with a triumph, but he was returning with troops.

With his military might Essex dreamed he could seize power. Essex
wanted the throne, and he persuaded himself that Elizabeth would hand
it to him by marriage. In September 1599 Essex landed in London. With
his troops he forced his way into the palace at Whitehall. He broke into
the Queen's bedroom and found a frightened, old, balding lady, un-
wigged and undressed, without any aid of cosmetic artifice. Such a royal
trespass—unprecedented in English history—was in itself a treasonous
act.

Elizabeth, though without her wig, kept her wits about her.[2] Some speculate that the Queen soft-talked Essex, assuring him of her desire to marry and share the throne with him.[3] Reportedly, she persuaded him to disband his troops, explaining that marriage under duress would erode the very popularity that would make him such a splendid ruler. The Queen, however, had no intention of marrying Essex. While Essex's men slowly dispersed, returning to their homes and families, Elizabeth pretended to stir the ashes of their old romance.

If she did promise Essex, she reneged and turned the Essex problem over to her ministers. Elizabeth may have loved the earl, but she loved the throne more. Her ministers would have liked to send Essex to the Tower for treason, but after more months of debate in early 1600 the Queen decided on a house arrest. Essex would be deprived of all his offices of state, and he would be under sworn oath not to leave his London house without permission.

By September 1600, Essex and Southampton had for months been chafing at their imprisonment and at Elizabeth's duplicity. Essex retaliated by hatching a plot. Conspirators with weapons concealed under their doublets would infiltrate the palace. Upon a signal the guards would be seized, to allow entry of Essex into the Queen's chamber.[4] While Essex forced Elizabeth to accede to his terms, his men were to arrest Cecil's son Robert, Bacon, and Raleigh for their treasonous counsel to the Queen.

Yet such a naked seizure of power depended on the sanction of popular support. For this, Southampton turned to Shakespeare. Could *Richard II* be staged again? Shakespeare's fellow actors doubted that the old chronicle could be dusted off and revived successfully, but Southampton guaranteed that partisans of Essex would pack the Globe Theatre.[5] Still, the actors hesitated to become treasonably involved—they were players, not plotters. A representative of Essex convinced them by doubling their wages for the performance, on Saturday afternoon, February 7, 1601.[6]

Before morning of that day, government spies learned of the plot. Guards were added in the palace and put on alert. Essex's men held back, awaiting a signal from the earl, who in turn was looking for some spark of popular support that he could fan into an uprising.

The play had to be that spark. At noon the faction favoring Essex gathered at Gunther's Inn, in London city, for a feast in anticipation. Afterwards, they rowed themselves across the Thames to the Globe, to see a play about the dethronement of an impotent monarch who was served by incompetent advisors.[7]

If a decade earlier Shakespeare had played the young Richard, some suggest that he now went on the stage to play the aging John of Gaunt.[8]

Shakespeare had an innate dignity on stage that suited him for such roles. A quiet audience listened to the old Duke's dying oration:

> This royal throne of kings, this sceptr'd isle,
> This earth of majesty, this seat of Mars,
> This other Eden, demi-paradise;
> This fortress built by Nature for herself
> Against infection and the hand of war;
> This happy breed of man, this little world,
> This precious stone set in the silver sea,
> Which serves it in the office of a wall,
> Or as a moat defensive to a house,
> Against the envy of less happier lands;
> This blessed plot, this earth, this realm, this England.

If Shakespeare did play Gaunt, applause surely greeted his rendition, as well as the entire show. But outside the Globe, Londoners did not lift their hands to take arms in behalf of Essex. At a time when almost all believed in the divine right of kings, the dethroning of a monarch, even in favor of a popular idol, seemed too drastic and dangerous.

Under Robert Cecil's orders, Essex and Southampton were captured and taken to the Tower. The actors who revived *Richard II* explained that they were simply taking advantage of a commercial opportunity.

A trial for treason followed, with Sir Francis Bacon as the prosecutor. Bacon, Essex's long-time friend, turned against his former mentor. As proof of a plot against the crown, Bacon would offer in evidence the play *Richard II*, which had encouraged the dethronement of the monarch and therefore was seditious.[9]

Bacon charged that Essex was guilty of high treason. The jury, composed of Edward de Vere, the Earl of Oxford; William Stanley, the Earl of Derby; and Sir Walter Raleigh, found Essex guilty and sentenced him to death. That fact alone should answer those who have the fanciful theory that Bacon, or Oxford, or Raleigh, or Derby was really the author of Shakespeare's plays, including *Richard II*. Would DeVere, Bacon, or Raleigh have condemned their own work? Would DeVere, or any adviser to the Queen, have risked losing his power by writing a play that he knew would be judged as treasonous?

During the trial the Queen withdrew to her private chambers at Whitehall. She was a stricken woman, torn between her love of Essex and her duty to England. As sovereign, she had at last decided that it was in the best interests of her country to let the sentence stand. In her room she sat alone as Essex, garbed in a black satin suit trimmed with white cuffs and with a crimson doublet underneath, mounted the scaffold. The drum-beat signaling the moment, and the slash and thump of the executioner's blade, sounded through her window.[10]

When Essex ascended the scaffold, Elizabeth had already started her slow descent to death. Although flashes of her robust personality were occasionally manifest, she had turned 70 and faced the specter of death.

NOTES

1. Peter Quennell, *Shakespeare: The Poet and His Background* (Cleveland: World, 1963), p. 229.

2. Quennell, *Shakespeare*, p. 230; Peter Levi, *The Life and Times of William Shakespeare* (New York: Holt, 1988), p. 201.

3. Quennell, *Shakespeare*, p. 230.

4. Joseph Quincy Adams, *A Life of William Shakespeare* (Boston: Houghton Mifflin, 1923), p. 316.

5. Marquette Shute, *Shakespeare of London* (New York: Dutton, 1949), p. 249.

6. Quennell, *Shakespeare*, p. 235.

7. Shute, *Shakespeare of London*, p. 249.

8. Clara Longworth de Chambrun, *Shakespeare: A Portrait Restored* (London: Holis & Carter, 1957), p. 230.

9. Ibid., p. 233.

10. Quennell, *Shakespeare*, p. 248; Shute, *Shakespeare of London*, p. 250.

CHAPTER EIGHTEEN

The Sovereign and Son Who Might Have Been

Now cracks a noble heart. Good night sweet prince.

Hamlet
act 5, scene 2

For Shakespeare it was also time for inward probing. A congenial and cheerful man, he was disturbed by the grim proceedings of 1601.[1] His hero Essex had been executed and his patron Southampton taken to the Tower, to await, perhaps, a similar fate.

Shakespeare's mind might have turned back to that other ordeal that had shattered him. The death of his son was more than five years passed, but its pain must have been still keenly felt. In those five years Shakespeare had become the nation's premier poet and playwright. Perhaps musing on both the young man and the king that might have been, he wrote what would be his masterpiece.

Even the title *Hamlet*, is an echo of his son's name. One writer, Clara Longworth de Chambrun, even states that occasionally he spelled his son's name Hamlet instead of Hamnet.[2]

The story of a prince who fails to avenge his father's murder was not new. *The Spanish Tragedy*, by Thomas Kyd, was one of London's most popular plays, even rivaling Shakespeare's *Titus Andronicus*. It is said Shakespeare himself had once played Kyd's protagonist, Hieronimo, who vows to the audience that he will have revenge.[3] Now Shakespeare, with his genius, reversed the character. Hamlet would be one who *cannot* take revenge. The psychological dimension that Shakespeare added made the drama the greatest in literature.

Shakespeare also moved the setting from Spain to Denmark. His old colleague Will Kempe had written him a letter from Denmark describing Elsinore Castle.[4] Kempe, now retired from the Burbage company, had been presenting his one-man show before royal audiences. He had been playing to the royal court in Copenhagen in 1595 when King James of Scotland visited to woo Anne, the Danish princess he would marry. In switching the backdrop from Spain to Denmark, Shakespeare could also change the title. He had discovered in Danish history a prince by the name of Amleth, son of King Horrendill of Jutland. By changing the name slightly, he could approximate and honor his own son's name.[5]

At one level the Lord of Elsinore is Essex. The indecision of Essex when the time was ripe for a strike applied to Shakespeare's Hamlet. The words of the world's most famous soliloquy could recall Essex, as he contemplated whether to seize the throne.

> To be, or not to be: that is the question:
> Whether 'tis nobler in the mind to suffer
> The slings and arrows of outrageous fortune,
> Or to take arms against a sea of troubles,
> And by opposing end them.

When Ophelia is describing Hamlet, she could be depicting the handsome Essex, who had struck such a presence in Elizabeth's court.

> The courtier's, soldier's, scholar's eye, tongue, sword:
> The expectancy and rose of the fair state,
> The glass of fashion and the mould of form,
> The observed of all observers.

But Essex was far from the complex character of Hamlet that Shakespeare etched with his poetic pen. The Prince of Denmark, who is a student intellectual from Wittenberg University, is the subtlest challenge for any actor. By turns Hamlet is impulsive and irresolute, compassionate and crude, manic and meditative. As a leader he is the idealist unable to come to grips with political reality. In some ways, Hamlet is a medieval version of the limousine liberal or paralyzed intellectual: he talks the language of the radical, but cannot turn his analysis into action.

On the other hand, Polonius, the state treasurer of Denmark, may be interpreted as a parody of Cecil, who held the same position under Queen

Elizabeth. Before he died in 1598, Cecil had written to his son Robert a manual of statecraft entitled "Precepts," which was a didactic tract.

In the play Polonius gives a little sermon full of truisms to his foppish son Laertes as he leaves for school in Paris. It is the most quoted lecture in history, though its reciters often forget Shakespeare's original ironic touch.

> And these few precepts in thy memory
> Look thou character. Give thy thoughts no tongue,
> Nor any unproportion'd thought his act.
> Be thou familiar, but by no means vulgar.
> Those friends thou hast, and their adoption tried,
> Grapple them to thy soul with hoops of steel.
>   . . .
> Give every man thine ear, but few thy voice:
> Take each man's censure, but reserve thy judgement.
> Costly thy habit as thy purse can buy,
> But not express't in fancy; rich, not gaudy.
>   . . .
> Neither a borrower nor a lender be:
> For loan oft loses both itself and friend,
> And borrowing dulls the edge of husbandry.
> This above all: to thine own self be true,
> And it must follow, as the night the day,
> Thou canst not then be false to any man.

Shakespeare would impart his own advice in *Hamlet*. A company of student players visits Elsinore Castle. Shakespeare, through Prince Hamlet, is the director who has supervised thousands of rehearsals and performances.

Speak the speech, I pray you, as I pronounced it to you, trippingly on the tongue: but if you mouth it, as many of your players do, I had as lief the town-crier spoke my lines. Nor do not saw the air too much with your hand, thus; but use all gently . . .

Shakespeare was denouncing the hams who overact their lines. Just possibly the actor Shakespeare might also have had in mind the clown performer of the Burbage troupe, Will Kempe, who was known for his exuberant renditions. Even his friend and colleague Richard Burbage occasionally overplayed his roles, though the acting company was known for its restraint. When Shakespeare says "trippingly," we remember Richard Burton's explanation of the way he conversationalized verse. Less accomplished actors performing Shakespeare's plays often draw breath at the end of the poetic line, and so cause a double break.[6]

Shakespeare, possibly speaking about Kempe, might also have been referring to the cant of political demagogues, who shout to make a point:

O, it offends me to the soul to hear a robustius periwig-pated fellow tear a passion to tatters, to very rags, to split the ears of the groundlings.

Shakespeare, an authority on acting and speaking, inserted into *Hamlet* a scene that would intrigue another kind of expert. King James of Scotland, who was the expected heir to the dying Elizabeth, had written a treatise on the supernatural.

In the first act, the ghost of King Hamlet appears before his son and in an eerie and distant voice tells how his brother Claudius murdered him and seduced his wife to gain the throne.

Ghost: But know, thou noble youth,
    The serpent that did sting thy father's life
    Now wears his crown.
Hamlet: O my prophetic soul! Mine uncle
Ghost: Ay, that incestuous, that adulterate beast,
    With witchcraft of his wit, with traitorous gifts,—
    O wicked wit and gifts, that have the power
    So to seduce!—and won to his shameful lust
    The will of my most seeming-virtuous queen.

When the Lord Chamberlain's Men enacted it, Richard Burbage would play Hamlet, but the specter was played by Shakespeare himself.[7] Shakespeare hoped to win acceptance from the King of Scotland, who was soon likely to become the King of England, and by making a part for himself in the first act, he may have been making sure King James got a glimpse of him. Some said the sherry-tippling Scottish King was known to fall asleep before a play ended. This was a real danger, since *Hamlet* is Shakespeare's longest play.

As it waited for one monarch to die and pondered the intentions of the next, London was a troubled city. In such unsettled times, none were more nervous than those in the city's entertainment industry, which included not only actors but clowns, jugglers, zookeepers, bearbaiters, boxers, wrestlers, and cockfight managers. All of these operated on the fringes of the law.

Shakespeare, no doubt, had heard conflicting stories about the head of the Stuart line in Edinburgh. If James liked theater, he never appeared in crowds. He was a scholar but was superstitious. He was the son of the beautiful Mary Queen of Scots, but it was also said that he was almost repulsive in appearance. His habits of hygiene did not enhance his regal image; if the rumors were to be believed, the Stuart king never bathed.

Shakespeare must have wondered what James knew about him and what his feelings were about the playwright's politics. What did the King of Scotland think about Shakespeare's play *Richard II*, and what was his reaction to the furor the deposition scene provoked? As the author of a treatise on the divine right of kings James would have been displeased, but as the son of Mary Queen of Scots, whom Queen Elizabeth had executed, he might not have been.

Shakespeare did know that James considered himself a scholar as well as a poet. Accordingly Shakespeare wrote *Hamlet*. He did not dash it off like one of his comedies—he carefully composed his most sublime drama. The poet Alfred Tennyson would call it "the greatest creation in literature."[8]

The poetry in *Hamlet* is unequalled. Shakespeare adapted scores of new words from French and Latin, to make it the richest in vocabulary of any of his plays.[9]

Actually, in writing his works Shakespeare would add over 1,700 words to the English language. Words such as frugal, generous, dire, lapse all appeared for the first time in Shakespeare's works. A deft mind faced by exigencies of meter would take the French word *modeste* and make it "modest," and from Latin he would appropriate the word obscene. Shakespeare had heard "rad" in the Kent county dialect and made it "road."

Sometimes he would add negative prefixes to coin new words, such as dishearten, invulnerable, and misplaced. Similarly he would append suffixes to mint such new words as baseless and countless. He changed a verb to a noun through a suffix to make accommodate into accommodation, employ into employment, and rely into reliance. To meet poetic demands, he filled *Hamlet* with such new words.

In *Hamlet* Shakespeare was striving for a masterpiece, and he achieved it. In a sense he was pursuing another potential patron, as he had done with Southampton almost a decade earlier.

Southampton, his former sponsor, had escaped the death sentence for his role in the Essex plot, but still remained in his Tower of London cell. It was Shakespeare's hope that the new King would pardon Southampton for his alleged crimes against the previous monarch. The 39-year-old English playwright awaited the disposition of the 37-year-old Scottish King.

On March 24, 1603, the old queen died in her sleep. Shakespeare, as a poet, was expected to compose an elegy. That he did not, in the face of contributions by so many lesser artists, was his own comment on the dead queen.[10]

The passing of Elizabeth was deeply mourned. The Virgin Queen had succeeded the reviled Mary, who had contracted her marriage bed to Philip, the king of Catholic Spain, England's most hated enemy. Her reign had brought nothing but defeat abroad and strife at home.

It is curious that England's greatest queen should have been held in such little esteem by England's greatest poet. Of course, one immediate reason may have been the execution of Essex, but a better explanation comes from Shakespeare in *Merry Wives of Windsor*—"upon familiarity will grow more 'contempt'." Many of the courtiers often watched Shakespeare and his fellow performers on stage. Similarly, the actors, with their many and often intimate ties to those in Whitehall, watched the Queen's advisers and courtiers up close in the public arena. Shakespeare had seen the face of power at too close a range.

As a playwright ahead of his time, Shakespeare created many strong women characters. His plays are filled with intelligent, ambitious, willful women who can outperform the men in either lawful or criminal objectives. Portia pleads in court, and Lady Macbeth murders for a crown.

Shakespeare saw young men act in the women's roles he created, but the greatest role he must have witnessed in his life was that of a woman playing a "man's" role in their own game of power politics. If Shakespeare did not join in the encomiums to Elizabeth, he had to respect her skill in statecraft.

NOTES

1. Peter Quennell, *Shakespeare: The Poet and His Background* (Cleveland: World, 1963), p. 278.

2. Clara Longworth de Chambrun, *Shakespeare: A Portrait Restored* (London: Holis & Carter, 1957), p. 255; Quennell, *Shakespeare*, p. 306.

3. Quennell, *Shakespeare*, p. 187.

4. Chambrun, *Shakespeare: Portrait*, p. 257.

5. Clara Longworth de Chambrun, *Shakespeare: Actor-Poet* (London: Appleton, 1927), p. 27.

6. Talk with the author at a radio interview in London in 1975.

7. Quennell, *Shakespeare*, p. 148.

8. Alfred Tennyson, quoted in Joseph Quincy Adams, *A Life of William Shakespeare* (Boston: Houghton Mifflin, 1923), p. 314.

9. Adams, *Life of Shakespeare*, pp. 310–11; Quennell, *Shakespeare*, p. 148.

10. Quennell, *Shakespeare*, p. 250; Adams, *Life of Shakespeare*, p. 355.

CHAPTER NINETEEN

The Playwright Finds a Patron

Then with Scotland first begin.

Henry V
act 1, scene 2

On June 4, 1603, James I of Scotland became James VI of England. Coincidentally, exactly 100 years earlier, Princess Margaret, the daughter of Henry VII and sister of the future Henry VIII, had married James IV of Scotland. It was the descent from Margaret Tudor that had awarded the English throne to James IV's grandson, James VI, and the House of Stuart.

As his carriage made its royal entry into London, all England greeted the arrival of the new King from Scotland with joy, anticipating a glorious new reign at the beginning of a grand new century. The Puritans found comfort because the new King had been raised as a Presbyterian by John Knox, while those who yearned for the return of the old religion reminded themselves that the new King's mother had been the fervently Catholic Mary Queen of Scots. London's community of writers took note of the fact that the new monarch was a scholar and a poet. Not the least hopeful of James's new subjects was Shakespeare.

At age 39 Shakespeare was wielding his poetic mastery to reign over the English theater. Now he hoped that the new King would give royal sanction to him and his acting company. The King might also free Shakespeare's old friend and sponsor, Southampton, from the Tower. After all, Southampton's family had been persecuted by Queen Elizabeth for advancing the cause of Mary Stuart.

Accordingly, Shakespeare tailored his next play to please the new King.[1] For material Shakespeare would look through his well-thumbed Holinshed, which recounted the history of England, Scotland, and Ireland in more than 3,000 pages.

Scotland naturally would be the focus of his studies. Scottish history is a tangled mess; the Scottish kings gained their thrones as much by battle as by bloodline. Sometimes the succession of a monarch was by a series of murders. These cabals and conspiracies offered a rich vein of dramatic material that could be mined for plots.[2] As Shakespeare sifted through the clan quarrels for the right storyline, a reference to Banquo must have made him stop and ponder. Banquo was the ancestor of the Stuart line.

Then he would have come across the battlefield killing of King Duncan by Macbeth. Even better, in the Holinshed account the death was predicted by witches. (The original Holinshed history featured as an illustration a crude woodcut, picturing Macbeth and Banquo on horseback encountering the three witches.) Shakespeare knew that King James was an authority on witchcraft; in 1597 the King had written a learned treatise on the black arts, entitled *Demonology*.[3]

But then later Shakespeare would read that Banquo had been involved in the plot to kill Duncan. For Shakespeare that must have posed a problem. He would resolve it with the use of an episode that was actually a century before King Duncan. A nobleman named Donald was egged on by his ambitious wife to murder a King Duff, while Duff was a guest in Donald's house. So Shakespeare would fuse the two plots together. The playwright's imaginative embroidery turned the battlefield death of Duncan into an assassination—a dastardly stabbing of the sleeping king.

One other fact in the Holinshed account must have troubled Shakespeare. Duncan, in his thirties, was almost the same age as Macbeth, and he had only been crowned a short time before his death. Actually, Duncan and Macbeth had been rivals for the throne. But by Shakespeare's pen Duncan was advanced in age to become "gracious Duncan," a kindly old man.

So Shakespeare wrote about Macbeth, the Thane of Cawdor, who thirsts for the throne of Scotland, which Duncan occupies. His wife encourages him in this ambition, but three witches offer cryptic warnings. While Duncan sleeps, Lady Macbeth completes the act of stabbing, which Macbeth has falteringly attempted. The two then kill Banquo, who is next in line of succession to the throne. The rest of the drama turns on the guilt of the Macbeths and the revenge on them by Malcolm, Duncan's son.

To keep a possibly drowsy King's full attention, Shakespeare penned his shortest tragedy. He opened it with a scene designed to capture the immediate attention of the King, who as we have seen was an expert on the black arts. The three witches appear, with talk of doom. They end the scene chanting:

> Fair is foul, and foul is fair.
> Hover through the fog and filthy air.

The witches, with their predictions, are an ever-looming presence in the play. The sleepwalking Lady Macbeth, moaning with guilt about the stabbing, must have reminded the audience of the recent Queen, who had put to death not only Essex but Mary Queen of Scots, her rival and James's mother.

Here's the smell of blood still: all the perfumes of Arabia will not sweeten this little hand. Oh, oh, oh!

Even the title of the tragedy might be interpreted as a play on the late Queen's name. "Mac" is the celtic prefix meaning from, out of, or of. So the title means "of Beth."

If Elizabeth is darkened by the linkage to Lady Macbeth, James is glorified through his ancestor Banquo. Banquo's historical involvement on the side of Macbeth is ignored, and the Banquo in the play is unselfish and noble.

In the beginning of the play, in Macbeth's presence, a witch cackles to Banquo about his fathering of the Stuart house. "Thou shall get kings, though thou be none." Later, the ghost of the murdered Banquo returns to haunt Macbeth (another appeal to King James, who considered himself an authority on ghosts).

The death of the maddened Lady Macbeth shakes Macbeth. When he says, "She should have died hereafter," among other things it is a wish that she could have borne him heirs. His present life and his gaining of the throne matters little to him; what he craves is an heir, to be the father of the kings who will rule long after he is dead. Shakespeare understood the need for a son and heir. Macbeth bemoans the sight of Banquo, with the line of his descendants to the seventh generation: "What! Will the line stretch out to the crack of doom? Another yet? A seventh? I'll see no more! And yet the eighth appears." (Mary Queen of Scots counted for the seventh Stuart generation, and her son James represented the eighth.) Macbeth sees the ghost of Banquo, who "doth treble scepters carry." Such was

Shakespeare's graceful tribute to James, who would rule England, Scotland, and Ireland. Some call *Macbeth* a propaganda play; if it was, it fulfilled its purpose.[4]

Yet if Macbeth was a political play, it nevertheless contained some of the best poetry Shakespeare had ever penned. Abraham Lincoln knew every word of the play by memory, and he used to mouth every word when he watched Edwin Booth play Macbeth in the Ford Theater during the Civil War. Lincoln, by the way, kept a copy of Shakespeare's tragedies on his White House desk. (The books beside it were the King James version of the Bible, the U.S. Constitution, and the U.S. Statutes).

For the often melancholy Lincoln, the soliloquies of Macbeth were favorite passages. This emotional rhetoric, which betrays the remorse of a mind racked by its self-doubts, struck a resonant chord with the president. Interestingly, in this play, which deals with kings and affairs of state, Shakespeare offers no orations. In that sense *Macbeth* is an exception. Instead, the declamations come in soliloquies. Unlike Prince Hamlet's intellectual musings, the outcries of Macbeth and Lady Macbeth are emotional and even sensual.

The most sublime soliloquy, and the favorite of Lincoln, was Macbeth's plaint that fate affords man's life not a thing worth mourning:

> Tomorrow, and tomorrow, and tomorrow,
> Creeps in this petty pace from day to day,
> To the last syllable of recorded time;
> And all our yesterdays have lighted fools
> The way to dusty death. Out, out, brief candle!
> Life's but a walking shadow, a poor player
> That struts and frets his hour upon the stage
> And then is heard no more; it is a tale
> Told by an idiot, full of sound and fury
> Signifying nothing.

The grateful King now adopted Shakespeare's company as his own. The Lord Chamberlain's Men would now be called the King's Men, and as such they could don for state occasions, royal crimson doublets adorned with the Stuart coat of arms. Shakespeare himself was appointed by the King a groom to the King's bed chamber. Sir George Hume, a Scottish courtier to the King, signed the order awarding Shakespeare the title of gentleman of the bed chamber in 1604.[5] Shakespeare was not the first poet to wear this livery; Geoffrey Chaucer had worn the royal badge of the household of Richard II.[6] Shakespeare was now acknowledged as Britain's premier poet, playwright, and artist.

NOTES

1. Peter Quennell, *Shakespeare: The Poet and His Background* (Cleveland: World, 1963), p. 299; Clara Longworth de Chambrun, *Shakespeare: A Portrait Restored* (London: Holis & Carter, 1957), p. 272; Peter Levi, *The Life and Times of William Shakespeare* (New York: Holt, 1988), p. 247. Levi writes that "the first play written specifically for the new reign of the King of Scotland in London was *Macbeth*."

2. Macbeth the High King. Scotland did not honor primogeniture or dynastic descent to the first born; the Scots elected their kings. While more democratic, the system resulted in assassinations by cousins or nephews. Macbeth was cousin to Duncan.

3. Quennell, *Shakespeare*, p. 300. In 1597 King James published a book on the black arts entitled *Demonology*.

4. Chambrun, *Shakespeare: Portrait*, p. 272, calls it "a propaganda play."

5. Tucker Brooke, *Shakespeare of Stratford* (New Haven, Conn.: Yale University Press, 1926), p. 48. "The account of Sir George Hume, Knight Master of the Great Wardrobe to the High and Mighty Prince, Our Gracious Sovereign Lord James . . . Red Cloth . . . William Shakespeare." Sir George Hume, who came from a Berwickshire family, was a favorite of James dating from his early manhood in Scotland. He shared with James a love of the theater. Sir George, incidentally, is an ancestor of the author.

6. Marquette Shute, *Shakespeare of London* (New York: Dutton, 1949), p. 263.

CHAPTER TWENTY

The Moor and Madness

Good Lord, what madness rules in
brain-sick men.

I Henry VI
act 4, scene 1

In those first years of King James, the King's Men basked in the limelight as England's star performing company. James Burbage had died, but his son Cuthbert had assumed the managerial duties. The Globe, which Cuthbert and the leading actors of the company, including Shakespeare, owned in shares, was the most prominent playhouse, and Shakespeare the most popular playwright. The Globe and the King's Men also featured London's most celebrated actor, Richard Burbage.

Burbage, a contemporary of Shakespeare, must have had to strain to play the role of the student prince in *Hamlet*. Just for the middle-aged Burbage to squeeze into Hamlet's tights must have been a problem, not to mention the task of plumbing the Dane's character—a complexity of contradictions.

The death of Burbage's father James and the departure of Will Kempe had no doubt solidified the friendship of Shakespeare and Burbage, who was eight years Shakespeare's senior. The Richard Burbage household, along with those of John Heminges and Henry Condell, two other actors and Globe shareholders of the company, were in the same Silver Street neighborhood where Shakespeare lived with the Mountjoys. Invitations to join their families for christenings and other celebrations gave Shakespeare a home away from home in London.[1]

In *Othello* and *King Lear*, Shakespeare would write two of Richard Burbage's greatest tragic roles. The audiences at the Globe now included many more women, whose tastes differed widely from those of the penny public that once had flocked into the old Theatre in Shoreditch. Indeed, at the Globe even the standees now had to cough up sixpence.

In *Othello* and *King Lear* Shakespeare offered up first an exotic scenario, then an eerie one, both of which would excite the jaded tastes of London's audiences.

In Elizabethan days the stage was stark. The audience did not expect a particular scene location to be graphically represented on stage—the place was readily accepted to be whatever the actors said it was. (King Richard II opens the second scene in act 3 saying, "Barkloughly castle call they this at hand?") The new clientele in the time of King James demanded more inventiveness on stage, however, and Shakespeare obliged them.

Othello would play in 1604 at the King's mansion at Whitehall, called Banqueting House. The play was staged in a specially built structure for masques and entertainment. Banqueting House was used to receive ambassadors when they presented their credentials and for an occasional royal dinner, such as the St. George's Day feast. The name Whitehall loosely referred to the royal residence, but actually it was the entire cluster of buildings that housed the offices of government.

Originally Whitehall had been called York House, the episcopal office and home of Thomas Wolsey, the Cardinal of York. As he expanded his power, Wolsey had enlarged his home and offices. When Henry VIII discharged Wolsey, the Tudor king moved his royal offices from Westminster to Whitehall, which was the new name Henry gave it.

Flanked by the coterie of courtiers that comprised the Royal set, King James and Anne, his Danish queen, seated themselves in Masque Room to watch Shakespeare's latest play, which featured Othello, a middle-aged North African general who falls in love for the first time with Desdemona, daughter of a Venetian nobleman.

Iago, his ambitious aide, sees in his commander's adoration of his bride the opportunity to drag him down. Envious of the general's fame, Iago, who is only an ensign, will sow jealousy as a weapon by which the old soldier will destroy himself. The difference in age as well as race is a fertile field in which to plant the noxious seed.

An ensign was the same as a staff adjutant. Often status-seeking families sought to place a younger son as a personal assistant to a high officer or court official. Shakespeare must have seen more than a few of these young

men, who had to submerge their own ambitions in flattering service to
their superiors.[2]

The type is not unknown today in bureaucratic corridors or corporate
suites: the conniver, a master of political intrigue and infighting who masks
his personal agenda in the guise of servile eagerness. As Iago describes
himself,

> Others there are
> who trimmed in forms and visages of duty
> Keep yet their hearts attending on themselves
> And throwing but shows of service on their lords
> Do well thrive by them, and when they have lined their coats
> Do themselves homage.

Iago sees a way to jump a rung up the political ladder:

> Cassio's a proper man: let me see now
> To get his place, and to plume up my will
> In double knavery—How, how?—Let's see
> After some time to abuse Othello's ear
> That he is too familiar with his wife.

Nowhere in Shakespeare's works is there a villain more treacherous than
Iago. He is more wicked than Aaron the Moor and cleverer than Richard III,
because his cleverness is his wickedness. Shakespeare had known a few
ambitious political aides like Iago. One of them, Henry Cuffe, a steward to
Essex, had betrayed his commander while pretending to be his loyal servant.

While young Iago has the cynicism of age, his general has the roman-
ticism of youth. The general and his adjutant contrast in character, just as
the two lovers contrast in complexion. Yet unlike actors in succeeding
centuries, Richard Burbage portrayed Othello as a Berber, not as a black.
After all, the ambassador of the Moroccan sultanate was a familiar figure
in the courts of Elizabeth and James. (England's fear of Spain had led
Elizabeth to court the country which lies to the south of Gibraltar.)

Still, prejudice against racial as well as religious intermarriage ran
strong, and again Shakespeare, as in *Merchant of Venice*, was ahead of his
time. The women, who now made up at least half of the relatively mature
audience at the Globe, were enthralled by the romance between the
middle-aged, turbaned general "of burnished complexion" and the young,
blonde Desdemona.

By offering a stolen handkerchief as evidence of a liaison between
Cassio and Desdemona, the wicked Iago, through insinuation, turns the

general against his young bride. In her supposed infidelity, Othello sees the part of himself that he has been taught to despise, the color of his skin.

Before Othello can destroy Desdemona physically, he first must destroy her psychologically. In a scene that must have titillated London ladies, Othello imagines that his wife's bedchamber is a room in a brothel, where Desdemona is the whore and her maid Emilia the madam.

> You, mistress
> That have the office opposite to Saint Peter
> And keep the gate of Hell.
> You, you, ay, you
> We've done our course, there's money for your pains:
> I pray you, turn the key and keep our counsel.

In the final scene the enraged Othello stabs Desdemona to death. Then, learning his mistake, he turns the knife on himself. The farewell speech attending the self-inflicted death may have been partially inspired by the words of Essex before his execution (even though Essex's crime was treason not murder).

> Speak of me as I am; nothing extenuate,
> Nor set down aught in malice: then must you speak
> Of one that loved not wisely but too well;
> Of one not easily jealous, but, being wrought,
> Perplex'd in the extreme.

Shakespeare had used an Italian novella as his basis for *Othello*, but he would delve into Holinshed's early history of Celtic Britain for *King Lear*, the theme of which has a contemporary ring: the emotional problems of age, compounded by abdication of power and the trauma of retirement. (Another source was the play *The True Chronicle, History of King Lear*, published in 1605—which also borrowed from Holinshed.)

Lear's daughter, Goneril, like so many in a younger generation, has not sympathy but scorn for his diminished status:

> Idle old man
> That still would manage those authorities
> That he has given away.

Lear is old age personified. Though based on a Celtic chieftain eight centuries previous, as father and king, Lear belongs to no time or country.

The abandoned monarch, against whom the forces of nature seem to be in league with his two cruel daughters, commands our sympathy. The dogs that bark at him are a supreme symbol of his impotence and the world's iniquity. Lear cries, "I am a man/more sinned against than sinning."

Superficially it might have seemed easier for the 50-year-old Burbage to play an old Lear than a young Hamlet. Yet the range of Lear's rhetoric demands both trumpet and strings. Lear can be as silken in some lines as he is thunderous in others.

Still, the real challenge for the actor was to compete with the stage effects. The play was staged at Whitehall in 1606. It is a wonder the palace did not blow down or burn up. A wind machine shook the audience, and also the stage.[3] Behind the stage, pieces of cut-up tin were hammered, to produce horrendous claps of thunder as a hundred candles flashed lightning. Never had viewers been subjected to such pyrotechnics.

Lear's outcries echo the lamentation of the wind amid a labyrinth of ruined masonry—all accompanied by the cannonade of thunder. The stupendous scene, which takes place after Lear is turned out of his daughter's palace into a storm, was a daring vision of the Inferno. Torrents of ice and water were poured down like rain upon the old man's defenseless head and on the companion-fool with him, who shivers as he tries to comfort his lord with jests and silly songs.

Beside Burbage as Lear was Robert Armin, who played the fool. The lanky Armin had succeeded the squat Kempe as the comic in the actors' company.[4] If Kempe in style was more the antic buffoon, Armin was a saturnine figure. Trained as a goldsmith, Armin was better educated than Kempe. His pale, haunted face and elegantly limp gestures must have suggested a Charlie Chaplin–type figure, not a clown.

In the play the deafening thunder and lightning flashes, together with the torrential rain (being poured from above from buckets through sieves), all express the tempest that tosses in the mind of the King. Hell, in the nature of the storm, manifests the spitefulness of his evil daughters— which seems to rise up in full panoply to crush the old man's pride, overthrow his wits, and break his heart.

When Shakespeare pictured in *King Lear* the rantings of a ragged old man, he may have had in mind the spectacle of William Hacket. This illiterate wretch shocked London in 1592 by mounting a little cart and prophesying to crowds the end of the world, unless England returned to the ways of justice. When he threatened to unloose plagues unless the Queen and her Privy Council resigned, he was executed.[5] Yet the idea that folly rules the world had been introduced by the writings of Erasmus of Rotterdam. Shakespeare inserts this belief into the vituperation of the mad king.

Lear, shorn of his trappings of power, begins to strip himself of his remaining rags, to man's true state of nakedness.

Thou art the thing itself: unaccommodated man is no more but such a poor, bare, forked animal as thou art. Off, off, you lendings, come, unbutton here.

Previous Shakespearean heroes had gone to death in royal state, but the sole dignity Shakespeare allows Lear is that of self-inflicted destitution, as he again rips off his garments. If Othello and Macbeth are men who fell to great depths from great heights, King Lear is one who rises from great depths to transcendent heights, beyond "the rack of this tough world."

NOTES

1. Marquette Shute, *Shakespeare of London* (New York: Dutton, 1949), p. 276.
2. Ibid.
3. Ibid.; Peter Quennell, *Shakespeare: The Poet and His Background* (Cleveland: World, 1963), p. 306.
4. Quennell, *Shakespeare*, p. 187.
5. Fantan O'Toole, *No More Heroes: A Radical Guide to Shakespeare* (Dublin: Raven Arts Press, 1890), p. 76.

CHAPTER TWENTY-ONE

The King's Man

The presence of a king engenders love
Amongst his subjects and his loyal friends.

I Henry VI
act 3, scene 1

King Lear in his rags on stage evoked a majesty that King James in all his regalia in Court could not muster. The Stuart king, according to some court critics, stuttered in his speech, slobbered from his mouth, and stumbled in his walk, dragging a gimpy leg.

The wags at Court whispered, "King Elizabeth has been followed by Queen James." Queen Bess, even in her last years, had held herself erect as she walked among her subjects, fixing them purposefully in the eye. King James, however, was fearful of crowds and avoided his subjects' eyes as if a glance might transmit the plague. An effeminate pedant, he was called "the wisest fool in Christendom."

Yet Shakespeare was loyal to this odd king who preferred his studies to his subjects. After all, soon after he was crowned, the Stuart monarch had freed Shakespeare's sponsor Southampton from the Tower. Soon after, James adopted Shakespeare's company as the King's Men. Shakespeare wanted to repay that royal patronage, and the curious play *Measure for Measure* was his offering.

Vincentio, the duke of Vienna in this play, is such a detached ruler that he quits his realm and delegates his duties to his Deputy Angelo. Angelo—

and incidentally, this would someday be the first Shakespearean role that the 20-year-old Oxford student Richard Burton played—is a

> proud man,
> Drest in a little brief authority,
> Most ignorant of what he's most assured.

The Duke, however, is clearly modeled after King James.

Shakespeare put the case for James in the words of the Duke, who says:

> I love the people,
> But do not like to stage me to their eyes;
> Though it do well, I do not relish well
> Their loud applause and Aves vehement;
> Nor do I think the man of safe discretion
> That does affect it.

With these words, Shakespeare makes such a weakness into a strength.

In the Duke's absence, the city seethes with political and moral corruption. The Duke's deputy Angelo masks his own moral rot by making a show arrest of Claudio as a fornicator. Angelo is the sort of puritanical zealot that offended Shakespeare. Shakespeare's own view of sensual sin is better expressed by Lucio: "Yes, in good sooth, the vice is of a great kindred; it is well allied; but it is impossible to extirp it quite, friar, till eating and drinking be put down." The playwright would surely have contempt for the Elmer Gantry–type antics of today's televangelist preachers. While publicly embracing morality with rigid enforcement, Angelo privately offers to commute the death sentence of Claudio if Claudio's sister, Isabella, consents to sleep with him.

Although Angelo and everyone else think the Duke is abroad, actually Vincentio stays behind in Vienna, disguising himself as a friar. The Duke watches the hypocritical officiousness of his deputy with disdain. He agrees with Isabella, who says:

> O, it is excellent
> To have a giant's strength; but it is tyrannous
> To use it like a giant.

In the end the grim play qualifies as a "comedy" because Isabella escapes the clutches of Angelo and the Duke returns to extricate Isabella from her complicated personal entanglements, with his judicious resolution of her difficulties.

King James must have appreciated the vindication *Measure for Measure* gave to his philosophy of kingship. Similarly, *Coriolanus*, written about 1608 and Shakespeare's last great tragedy, did, in a sense, also defend the Stuart foreign policy.

At a time when the far-flung Spanish fleet was throttling the expansion of English merchant trade, there was a public outcry for James to take up arms against the Spanish tyranny at sea.

In the pages of Plutarch, Shakespeare found the character Coriolanus. The fastidiousness of the Duke in *Measure for Measure*, which robbed him of any relish for the "aves vehement" of the people, is replicated in Coriolanus's scorn for all "acclamations hyperbolical." Despite their contrasting personalities, both Coriolanus, the savage warrior, and James, the bookish king, are contemptuous of the popular lust for war.

> You souls of geese
> That bear the shapes of men.

Against his better judgment, Coriolanus gives in to his mother's pleas to accept the consulship of Rome. The adulation of the crowd turns to scorn when he refuses to lead his country into war once again with the Volsci. Coriolanus cannot bow to the whim of the mob. Here is the conservatism of Shakespeare, who was as percipient as an Edmund Burke about the duty of an elected leader to give his best judgment, and not just reflect the sentiment of the crowd.

> Where gentry, title, wisdom
> Cannot conclude but by the yea and no
> Of general ignorance—it must omit
> Real necessities and give way the while
> To unstable slightness. Purpose so barred, it follows,
> Nothing is done by purpose.

Coriolanus is banished by the Senate, and he takes exile with the Volsci, whom he once vanquished. When war does come, Coriolanus fights, but at the head of the Volsci army. He conquers Rome and is urged by the Volsci commanders to lay waste the city that wronged him. Heeding the cries of his mother Volumnia, he spares Rome but signs his own death warrant in doing so. He dies bravely defying the angry Volsci soldiers.

Coriolanus is the last of Shakespeare's grand tragedies. Some mistakenly see Coriolanus as monstrously arrogant, yet this character is victim not so much of his pride as his principles. Coriolanus's political rectitude, however, was less interesting to theatergoers than Macbeth's ambition or Othello's jealousy.

Though only in his mid-forties, the playwright poet found his energies waning. He ransacked the pages of Plutarch for two more plots—*Timon of Athens* and *Antony and Cleopatra*.

Perhaps in *Timon of Athens* Shakespeare also had in mind his new patron King James. Favorites, who are the curse of any court, bothered even a royalist like Shakespeare. In his plays Shakespeare directs some of his bitterest scorn on such courtiers and aides, like Caesar's Decius and Othello's Iago. There had been a plethora of favorites in the Hampton Palace of Elizabeth, but they became a plague in the Whitehall of James. Elizabeth had known how to manipulate her courtiers, but James often appeared to be their victim.

The title character in *Timon of Athens*, like King James, is a generous prince with kindly intentions. He is served by flattering lords and false friends, who exploit his benevolence until his riches are exhausted. Bereft of friends and fortune, Timon retreats from the city of Athens to the country. There he discovers gold, with which he pays whores and bandits to destroy the society that once praised him. *Timon of Athens* is not a tragedy but a bitter comedy—a comedy of bad manners.

Shakespeare's story of Antony, Caesar's successor, was more popular than *Timon of Athens* or *Coriolanus*. If in *Coriolanus* the theme was lust for war, in *Antony and Cleopatra* it is lust itself. Like a modern Edward VIII, Antony risks his throne for the love of a foreign woman. Enobarbus says of her:

> Age cannot wither her, nor custom stale
> Her infinite variety: other women cloy
> The appetites they feed, but she makes hungry
> Where most she satisfies.

Coriolanus and Antony were both brave soldiers. The first is destroyed by the influence of a strong mother, and the second is ruined by a seductive woman. In creating Cleopatra, perhaps Shakespeare had in mind both the Mrs. Lanier of his twenties and the Mrs. Davenant of his middle age. The dark-haired Egyptian queen seems a combination of the flirtatious Emilia and the bright-minded Jane.

Despite the appeal of this torrid romance, Globe Theatre of the King's Men found itself waning. Much of the upscale crowd that used to frequent the Globe were now filling the seats at the rival theater, the Blackfriars.

Part of the appeal of the Blackfriars was comfort. It had a thatched roof to shelter the patrons from rain, and hot air heating to warm the audience on chilly days.

In a sense, Shakespeare's company was a victim of its own success. The patronage of James I had taken theater from the quasi-legal to the royally sanctioned. The minimum charge at the Blackfriars Theatre was six times that at the Globe Theatre.[1]

If the tradesmen, apprentices, and lawyers had made up the bulk of the audience that once enjoyed Shakespeare's chronicles, it was the upper middle class, rich merchants and their wives, who ten years later were paying to see *Othello* and *Lear*. Before the start of the seventeenth century, a woman at the theater was a daring exception, but in the early years of the new century, "matinee matrons" might comprise most of the audience.

Blackfriars was located near Fleet Street, in the posh residential section of London, within walking distance of these women's houses, but to get to the Globe, a playgoer had to either cross the Thames by boat or take the long way around via London Bridge.

Even before the accession of James, the Globe had witnessed the growing popularity of the Boys' Theatre, which was housed at Blackfriars. The choirboys of St. Paul's Cathedral and the Queen's Chapel Royal had for some time been staging plays there for members of the Court and wealthy Londoners. The boys, chosen for their voice, boarded at a church annex, received classroom instruction, and performed their singing duties at chapel services. The choirboys' masque or revue, which had once been an occasional holiday entertainment, was now a tradition. For their shows a private hall was rented in the exclusive Blackfriars area.

By the time of King James, the choirboys were having some of their musicales written by established poets and playwrights, such as John Marston, Thomas Dekker, and George Chapman. They staged their performances in the Blackfriars Theatre, which the Burbages had renovated in 1597 but had not been allowed to occupy. The young actors now posed a "professional" threat to the commercial acting companies.

The acting company that comes to Elsinore in *Hamlet* is one suffering from the competition of the Boy Actors. Rosencrantz explains to the prince why the repertory company is traveling in Europe: "There is, Sir, an eyrie [choir loft] of children, little eyases, that cry out on the top of question and are most tyrannically clapped [applauded] for 't. These are now the fashion, and so berattle the common [commercial] stages." Hamlet, amazed, asks, "What, are they children? who maintains 'em?"

What was galling to the Burbage family was that they actually owned the Blackfriars Theatre, where the choir school, calling itself the Boys' Theatre, was now staging its productions. When James Burbage's dream for a year-round covered theater in the exclusive section of London had collapsed under a storm of neighborhood protests, his son Cuthbert had rented out the now vacant theater to the Boys' Theatre. Since the choirboys were not professional actors, they could circumvent the "zoning" restrictions, which the wealthy residents of Blackfriars had enacted with the help of their Puritan allies in the Privy Council. (One Puritan parson had charged that the theatrical performance would drown out the afternoon sermon and prayers in the local parish church.) The residents of Blackfriars had blocked the Burbage actors from playing in their neighborhood, citing the need to uphold standards of public decency. Yet it would be the Anglican choirboys who would overstep the bounds of decency, at least in the mind of King James.

In the summer of 1608, the St. Paul's Cathedral choirboys staged a skit portraying a bibulous and bumbling king. Enraged, James closed down the Boys' Theatre and allowed his "own" company, the King's Men, to take over Blackfriars as their winter home.[2] Although the Boys' Company no longer performed on the Blackfriars stage, their saucy musical skits would leave an imprint on Londoners' tastes.

NOTES

1. S. H. Burton, *Shakespeare's Life and Stage* (Edinburgh: W. & R. Chambers, 1989), p. 194.

2. Joseph Quincy Adams, *A Life of William Shakespeare* (Boston: Houghton Mifflin, 1923), pp. 404–5.

CHAPTER TWENTY-TWO

The Squire and His Ladies

Thou art my flesh, my blood, my daughter.

King Lear
act 2, scene 4

At the same time as the King's Men moved their main base of operations from the Globe to Blackfriars, Shakespeare left Silver Street to spend most of his time in Stratford.[1] The Londoner had become a country gentleman. No doubt his father's death in 1604 was a reason for his return; now he was head of the Shakespeare family.

Shakespeare had bought New Place ten years earlier and had leased it out to his friend he called his cousin, the lawyer Thomas Greene.[2] In buying New Place, Shakespeare had bought more than a house; he had purchased a history and a heritage.

The manor house had been built in the last years of Henry VIII by Sir Hugh Clopton, the one-time Lord Mayor of London.[3] Before the prominence of Shakespeare, Clopton had been Stratford's most successful son. As will be recalled from Chapter 1, he had endowed the royal grammar school, which Shakespeare attended as a youth, and had erected the graceful bridge that spans the Avon.

Shakespeare had bought the rundown mansion at a bargain from the Combe family, who had succeeded the Cloptons. But it turned out to be not so cheap. A Combe owner had been convicted of murder, and for such a crime the law stated that the murderer's estate should escheat to the Crown.

Shakespeare retained Greene to clear the title to New Place in a series of lawsuits. Then, in addition to the legal costs of perfecting his title to the house, he had the additional expense of restoring it to its former glory.

It is interesting to note that Churchill, like Shakespeare, chose to restore an old house instead of building a new one. Shakespeare at New Place and Churchill at Chartwell both kept the old names of their century-old manors and made improvements as well as repairs, but maintained their houses' original character.

Both Shakespeare and Churchill yearned for the verities of simpler times. In Elizabethan London, new money and new fortunes had uprooted the old codes and duties of chivalry. Merchants were replacing knights. Francis Bacon and Walter Raleigh may have embodied the inquiring mind and adventurous spirit of the Elizabethan Renaissance, but the country squire in Shakespeare saw them as parvenus (even if he was one himself).

To Shakespeare the feudal age had all the mysticism of an ancient castle, which the new materialism with all its profits and gold could not outshine. Like Churchill, who would rue the industrialism of the twentieth century, Shakespeare saw unwholesome changes in Renaissance London and sought for himself the rustic virtues of country life. New Place for Shakespeare, like Chartwell for Churchill, was an endeavor as well as an escape. They would rebuild and restore.

The radical tears down and builds anew, but Shakespeare distrusted the ideologue. Though he supported the attempt of Essex to revive the monarchy, he would have opposed Oliver Cromwell, whose zealous Republicanism some forty years later would uproot it. Similarly, Churchill, in his *History of the English-speaking Peoples*, could admire Cromwell but reject his political extremism: "If in a tremendous crisis Cromwell's sword had saved the cause of Parliament, he must stand before history as a representative of dictatorship and military rule, who with all his qualities of soldier and statesman, is in lasting discord with the genius of the English race."[4] Shakespeare wrote of "the doctrine of ill doing."

In *II Henry VI* he makes the revolutionary Jack Cade a villain, and in *Julius Caesar* he describes the savage excesses that can result from the noblest intentions of someone like Brutus. In *Troilus and Cressida* he writes:

> The enterprise is sick! . . .
> Take but degree away, untune that string, And, hark, what discord follows!
>   Each thing meets
> In mere oppugnancy.

Shakespeare was not a revolutionary but a restorer. His work at New Place was conservation, and his philosophy was that of a conservative. At New Place the result was a stately house of brick and timber that presided over about an acre of land, which included two barns and a garden. The frontage of the three-story, five-gabled house extended more than sixty feet, while the middle portion was at least seventy feet deep. At a time when each fireplace was a taxed luxury, New Place had at least ten. The handsomest house in town was appropriate to Shakespeare's status as a squire.[5]

The playwright's special pride must have been his garden in the rear. There on a sunny day Shakespeare probably sat on the stone bench underneath the growing mulberry tree, and penned his next plays as he drank in the scents of his thyme and rosemary plants. If it rained, Shakespeare might have sat facing out the bay window on the side of the house that overlooked the garden. In *Richard II* the gardener says:

> O what pity is it
> That he had not trimmed and dressed his land
> As we this garden!

If the liberal often sees himself as an architect, the conservative sees himself as a gardener, carefully cultivating the nation and society as a living thing. In the same play Shakespeare also described England as "a sea-walled garden."

For Shakespeare, however, gardening was much more than a leisure activity; it was an art, and one that had always stirred his imagination. His plays abound in garden and orchard images, figuratively embodying emotions and ideas. In gardening he habitually found symbols to represent the subtle interplay of nature and nurture in human affairs.

For a squire the only thing more important than his house is his heirs. Shakespeare had two daughters: Susanna, the elder, and Judith, the twin sister of the dead Hamnet. Susanna would give him a granddaughter, Elizabeth, in 1608. The birth must have softened the blow of losing his mother the same year, when Mary Arden Shakespeare was put to rest beside her husband John in the family tomb at Holy Trinity Church.

New Place in Stratford, where he was surrounded by his women kinfolk, was a far cry from theater life in London, which was totally a man's world. The sunny, herb-scented garden,[6] where he and his wife might visit with his daughters, was in strong contrast to the musty, ale-filled haunts of such taverns as the Mermaid, where Shakespeare used to dine with fellow writers.

Women now filled Shakespeare's world, and women would be the dominant figures of his next two plays. The two heroines in *Cymbeline* and *The Winter's Tale* would have roles that might have attracted a Judith Anderson or a Katherine Hepburn.

The two plays were neither comedy nor tragedy. Strip away the lush poetry and you might see the mushy plot of a handkerchief movie melodrama of the 1940s, in which because of some mistimed meeting or other misadventure a romance is aborted, even if, in the end, love triumphs over heartbreak.

Shakespeare had established his name with the chronicle plays, then fended off the Jonson competition with comedies, and finally reached his dramatic zenith with tragedies such as *Hamlet* and *Lear.* Now, in the sunset of his life, he would create for his acting company a new genre to hold the women patrons, whose attendance had made the Boys' Theatre at Blackfriars so popular.

Perhaps it was only to be expected that Shakespeare would turn to the treatment of women, since for the first time in his life he was mostly in the company of the opposite sex. In Stratford he must have found the company of his older, albeit ailing, wife a source of comfort and security. Anne Hathaway may have never approved of the theater, but she no doubt basked in her status as mistress of Stratford's greatest manor house. And no doubt she preferred to see her husband more as a squire than as a star playwright. She was, after all, Mistress Shakespeare, the wife of Stratford's most famous citizen.

Yet Shakespeare's favorite companion was probably his elder daughter Susanna, a woman who was described by contemporaries as "witty beyond her sex."[7] Though Susanna was a Puritan like her mother, she was literate and bright. She and her husband, Dr. John Hall, a graduate of Queens College, Cambridge (B.A. 1594, M.A. 1597)[8] entertained widely in their set of educated professionals.

Shakespeare's younger daughter was Judith, the twin of the dead Hamnet. If Susanna had inherited her father's mind, Judith may have uncomfortably reminded Shakespeare of his sensual side. To Shakespeare's dismay, she did not bother to learn to read or write. Though indolent, Judith was also of an independent mind, choosing not to settle down and marry the kind of man her parents would have chosen.[9]

Neither the witty Susanna nor the wayward Judith were women who could be called demure or deferential in the company of men. After all, their father had not been a continuing presence in their formative years. At this time of their lives, Shakespeare imparted almost an avuncular presence. The picture of Shakespeare that comes to mind is taken from the Chandos portrait (often said to have been painted by Richard Burbage), made when he was in his mid-forties. The dome-like head suggests wisdom, the bright eyes promise keenness of observation, and the trim mustache and goatee hint of artistic flair.

A perceptive and enthusiastic listener, Shakespeare always attracted women. His relationships with women may not have been impeccable, but he was not a womanizer. If he could not be quite characterized as a feminist he was, at least through his plays, sympathetic to the potential of women. Portia had the brains to win the court case and save Antonio. Lady Macbeth had the nerve to carry out the murder her husband had started. Beatrice, in *Much Ado About Nothing*, could have been an early version of Jane Austen's Elizabeth Bennett, and it is interesting to note that in an age when wife-beating was the rule and not punished by the courts, the nagging Kate never had a hand laid on her by Petrucchio in *Taming of the Shrew*. In *All's Well that Ends Well*, Shakespeare again revealed sympathy for women, when Diana says "tis a hard bondage to become the wife of a detesting lord".

In both *Cymbeline* and *The Winter's Tale*, a strong woman is wronged by a weak and insecure husband. Imogen, the daughter of King Cymbeline, is the victim of her husband Posthumus, who wagers on his wife's chastity during his absence and then fails to believe in her innocence. In *The Winter's Tale* Hermione is accused falsely of adultery. She departs, is presumed dead, and her baby daughter is abandoned exposed on a distant coast.

The plots of the two plays are roughly similar, and both were written to celebrate royal marriages in the family of King James.[10] In the first, Shakespeare seems to be experimenting to please a changing audience, but in the second, he seems to be experimenting to please himself.

Cymbeline takes a Celtic Queen mentioned in Holinshed's history and submits her to a bedroom trick recounted before in Boccaccio's *Decameron*. Specifically, the would-be seducer Iachimo (a name deliberately suggestive of the wicked Iago) hides himself in a chest carried into Cymbeline's bedchamber. The plot of the innocent wife is a fairy tale adorned by rich poetry. At the end Posthumus begs for his wife's forgiveness, saying he should die for his crime. Imogen answers:

I'll sweeten the sad grave: thou shalt not lack
The flower that's like thy face, pale primrose, nor
The azure barebell, like thy veins, nor the leaf of eglantine
Whom not to slander
Our sweetend not thy breath

Perhaps Shakespeare was drinking in his own garden when he wrote those lines. The upper class ladies loved it, but it would not have excited the penny standees in the old Theatre. They might have yearned instead for the battle orations of *Richard III* or *Henry V.*

To please the matinee matrons who loved the fare of the Boys' Theatre, Shakespeare opened with an elegy choral song and later offered a dirge, to be played at the supposed death of Imogen.

But when the ladies left the performance they were more likely talking about the stage effects than humming bars from the play's musical scores. In the play a vision is acted out in which Posthumus imagines that the god Jupiter descends from heaven. Jupiter on invisible wires floats down on an eagle from above the audience's view, hurling a flashing thunderbolt. Such a feat of stagecraft had never before been attempted. The new theatrical tastes demanded tricks, and Shakespeare, who was a stage manager as well as an actor and playwright, obliged them. When it was performed over a half-century later, *Cymbeline* would be the pet play of King Charles II. And two centuries later, when the poet laureate, Alfred Lord Tennyson died, the book by his bed was opened to *Cymbeline*—his favorite play.[11]

If poets and monarchs liked *Cymbeline*, it is *The Winter's Tale* that today invites the attention of professors and Shakespearean scholars. In Shakespeare's own time, Ben Jonson would attack the play for its shoddy scholarship and blatant assault on the classical rules. Jonson hated the play, but the matrons loved the ballet, dances, and songs.

There is no more jealous man in literature than Leontes in *The Winter's Tale*. Once becoming jealous, Othello could go mad, but the jealousy of Leontes is madness from the start. Leontes finds his wife guilty of adultery with Polixenes, the King of Sicily. Hermione and her baby daughter, the alleged issue of the illicit liaison, go into hiding.

The coast is that of Bohemia. Jonson would write that any idiot should have known that Bohemia does not border the sea! But what angered Jonson even more was the play's lapse of time and switch of setting—two cardinal sins in the classical canons of dramatic unity.

The play switches from Sicily to Bohemia and back to Sicily again. Sixteen years elapse from the time of banishment to the time of reconciliation. In the meantime, the abandoned baby Perdita (Lost One) becomes a beautiful shepherd girl wooed by the prince and son of Polixenes.

In *Winter's Tale* the gardener in Shakespeare reappears. He treats the audience to an argument between Perdita and Polixenes about the use of plant breeding, which is seen to symbolize two lovers' two different natures and backgrounds.

To show the audience that 16 years have passed, Shakespeare introduces a new figure to literature: Father Time appears with a beard and scythe, holding an hourglass in which the sands of 16 years have run out. We are reminded of the movie device of calendar pages that flip past, showing a passage of years.

Shakespeare knew his friend and rival Jonson would be enraged by the device. So in a playful dig he inserted the most curious stage direction in all literature: "Exit all pursued by a bear." In the play a bear chases from the stage the shepherds who found the lost baby Perdita.

Some say that Shakespeare rented a tame bear from the next-door Bear Garden to run on stage in some of the play's first performances.[12] The bear could have represented the ursine Jonson, who because of his literary credo would have liked to run the play off the stage and out of England!

We can only imagine the shrieks of the matinee matrons as the beast lumbered across the stage. But what lingered in the women's thoughts after the play was not their fright at seeing the bear, but their sighs at watching a husband find his wife even more attractive after 16 years.

At the end of the play, Leontes sees a statue of his wife. She is not as she was, but as she is, 16 years older, with more wrinkles and lines. He gazes at the statue and realizes that he is even more in love than when he married her. As he cries out for forgiveness, his wife Hermione steps down from the pedestal. It is a tricky bit of stage magic, not only making the boy dressed in the woman's role look 16 years older, but also making him resemble an alabaster statue. At a time when women were objects diminished in value by age, Shakespeare was making a plea for the value of womanhood.

NOTES

1. Marquette Shute, *Shakespeare of London* (New York: Dutton, 1949), pp. 240–42.

2. Joseph Quincy Adams, *A Life of William Shakespeare* (Boston: Houghton Mifflin, 1923), p. 255.

3. Shute, *Shakespeare of London*, pp. 186–87.

4. Winston Churchill, *History of the English-speaking Peoples*, vol. 2 (New York: Dodd, Mead, 1956), p. 316.

5. Adams, *Life of Shakespeare*, pp. 252–53.

6. Peter Quennell, *Shakespeare: The Poet and His Background* (Cleveland: World, 1963), p. 322.

7. Adams, *Life of Shakespeare*, pp. 394–96. "Susanna seems to be the father's favorite. . . . This favorite daughter."

8. Peter Levi, *The Life and Times of William Shakespeare* (New York: Holt, 1988), p. 264.

9. Clara Longworth de Chambrun, *Shakespeare: A Portrait Restored* (London: Holis & Carter, 1957), pp. 369–70.

10. Adams, *Life of Shakespeare*, pp. 415–16.

11. Ibid., p. 416.

12. Quennell, *Shakespeare*, p. 323.

CHAPTER TWENTY-THREE

An Artist's Adieu

The web of our life is of a mingled yarn, good and ill together; our virtues would be proud, if our faults whipped them not; and our crimes would despair, if they were not cherished by our virtues.

All's Well that Ends Well
act 4, scene 3

In 1610 the 46-year-old Shakespeare was still the preeminent figure of English theater, but physically he was waning. He had given up acting with the King's Men when he returned to Stratford to take up his life as squire and country gentleman. Though his old colleagues, such as Richard Burbage, Henry Condell, and John Heminges were still acting, Shakespeare had withdrawn from the hectic theater life.

Shakespeare sold off the shares he held in the Globe and Blackfriars theaters. The new double team of Francis Beaumont and John Fletcher, along with Ben Jonson, were now providing most of the scripts for the King's Men.[1] There was no pressure for Shakespeare to turn out a new drama, nor did he have any desire. New play ideas were not bubbling in his head. His old sponsor Southampton, however, would induce him to change his mind.[2]

A few years earlier King James had released the earl from his cell in the Tower and had sent instead Sir Walter Raleigh, who sentenced Essex, to the same prison. The one-time favorite of Elizabeth was considered a political foe by the Stuart king. In a delicious irony, so typical of the political infighting of the Court, Raleigh would yield much of his holdings to Southampton, whose old cell he was now occupying. Southampton had been banished to the Tower and barely escaped the executioner's axe. The freed Southampton now took over Raleigh's principal venture, the Virginia Corporation. Raleigh, it will be remembered, had brought tobacco to Elizabethan England. King James disliked Raleigh, and also the smoking habit he had introduced. Said James, "Tobacco is a dirty weed. I hate it."

Raleigh's experiment in Virginia in the 1580s had apparently ended in the massacre of the Virginia settlers. Southampton attempted to breathe life into the colony-to-be, which Raleigh had founded in the name of the Virgin Queen, Elizabeth.

With Southampton's backing, a Captain Gosnell in the ship *Concorde* had discovered and named the James River in 1605. Four years later Southampton dispatched a fleet to begin a new settlement there. The putative leaders of the new colony, Lord Delaware, Thomas Gates, and Sir George Sommers, all sailed in one boat, the *Sea Venture*. The hapless ship was separated from the rest of the convoy when it ran into what we now call the Bermuda Triangle, and it was wrecked on the coast of a small sandy bay in Bermuda. The adventurers lived for a few months on the island and were able to construct a boat and rejoin the other colonists in Virginia.

The account by one of the survivors triggered an idea for a play for Shakespeare. The result was *The Tempest*. The Bermudas are even mentioned in the play:

> Thou call'dst me up at midnight to fetch dew
> From the still-vexed Bermoothes.

The prison years had matured Southampton. The Virginia project over which he had assumed control captured his energies, as pursuit of women and patronage of poetry had in his youth.[3] As an enthusiast for Virginia, Southampton introduced John Rolfe's wife, the Princess Pocahontas, to King James. Southampton was a convert to the New World mission, and Shakespeare honored that interest in *The Tempest*—"O brave new world/That has such people in't." As Southampton years earlier had enlisted Shakespeare's poetic pen to advance the cause of Essex, now he wanted Shakespeare to promote Virginia and its commercial possibilities.

Such was the origin of *The Tempest*. It was Shakespeare's last play, or at least the last play solely written by him. In fact, with the possible exception of *Midsummer Night's Dream*, it is about the only play not based on Holinshed or Plutarch, or using another writer's plot. The story is original with Shakespeare. He serves up an ocean voyage, a storm, a shipwreck, and a magic island.

Again Shakespeare employed the stage tricks that the more sophisticated Jacobean audiences had come to expect. It is conjectured that the ship glided on blue canvas, which was rippled by vigorous shakings from offstage. Stage innovations, such as flashing for lightning and clapping for thunder, threaten the ship. Later Juno's throne descends from the skies, and Ariel, the fairy sprite, appears suspended from the air. A sour Ben Jonson would attack *Tempest* for its excess in stagecraft.

The story was simpler than the stage set. A Duke, ousted by his brother in Naples, sails away and is shipwrecked on an idyllic island, where he establishes an ideal commonwealth. The name of the Duke is Prospero, which in itself was a plug for Southampton's business venture in the New World (even though this is a fictional island that has no geographic designation).

Prospero, with his wand and knowledge of astrology and the black arts, creates for his daughter Miranda a magic realm, even though he has to fight off the savagery of a native, Caliban (a phonetic anagram of "cannibal"). Perhaps Shakespeare was alluding to published reports of the human-eating Carib Indians in the Caribbean Islands.

Some see in *The Tempest* an allegory of his own farewell. Shakespeare's pen, like Prospero's wand, had created a world of make-believe. When Prospero gives up his magic rod, is Shakespeare saying goodbye?

> I'll break my staff,
> Bury it certain fathoms in the earth,
> And deeper than did ever plummet sound
> I'll drown my book.

Shakespeare, who had put in kings and nobles' mouths so many orations, would now write one for the dramatic artist. The audience no doubt caught the allusion to the Globe Theatre.

> Our revels now are ended. These our actors,
> As I foretold you, were all spirits, and
> Are melted into air, into thin air;
> And, like the baseless fabric of this vision,
> The cloud-capp'd towers, the gorgeous palaces,
> The solemn temples, the great *globe* itself,
> Yea, all which it inherit, shall dissolve,
> And, like this insubstantial pageant faded,
> Leave not a rack behind.

Prospero closes this speech with the distillation of Shakespeare's philosophy:

> We are such stuff
> As dreams are made on; and our little life
> Is rounded with a sleep.

The play is at the same time realistic and fantastic. Among its characters are men, supermen, kings, drunkards, lovers, monsters, and fairies. Shakespeare's last comedy is a waking dream made up of many separate visions. Prospero is dreaming of power and knowledge; Miranda and Ferdinand of love; Stephano and Trinculo of their now-found kingdom; Sebastian and Antonio, the conspirators, of treachery and self-advancement.

The play was staged at the Great Banqueting House at Whitehall on November 1, 1611, to usher in the revels of the season. Some even speculate that, as a special favor to King James, Shakespeare might have returned to the stage one last time, to play Prospero.

King James liked the play so much that he ordered *Tempest* to be performed on the same feast day the next year to celebrate the arrival of Frederick, the elector of the Palatinate, to betroth James's beautiful daughter Elizabeth. The sudden death of her brother Prince Henry, who died from a chill incurred while playing tennis, canceled the performance. The wedding of Elizabeth and Frederick would take place the following year in 1613 on Valentine's Day. *The Tempest* featured the marriage of Ferdinand to Miranda, the daughter of Prospero, and thus was considered ideal for the marriage occasion.

It was a time for rejoicing in London. Elizabeth was a popular princess who seemed to combine the intelligence of her godmother, the old Queen and her namesake, and the beauty of her grandmother, Mary Queen of Scots.

If starring as Prospero in his farewell performance would have been exhilarating, it would also have been enervating for the 49-year-old Shakespeare. He was feeling the ebbing of his tide of life. Even the three-day journey from Stratford to London must have been tiring. The trips now, however, were more like triumphant processions, as the noted actor and poet was often feted along the way by old admirers and friends.

Even after *Tempest* ceased performance, Shakespeare would still make an occasional journey to London—sometimes to fulfill some ceremonial obligations at Court. Although he was no longer that active in theater, his closest friends were still those of the King's Men.

NOTES

1. Marquette Shute, *Shakespeare of London* (New York: Dutton, 1949), pp. 303–4.

2. Clara Longworth de Chambrun, *Shakespeare: A Portrait Restored* (London: Holis & Carter, 1957), pp. 338–39.

3. Clara Longworth de Chambrun, *Shakespeare: Actor-Poet* (London: Appleton, 1927), pp. 230–31.

CHAPTER TWENTY-FOUR

Goodbye, Globe

Bare ruined choirs, where late the sweet birds sang.

Sonnet 73

In London Shakespeare was still the giant of the theater, but in Stratford he was the gentleman of New Place. He preferred the latter. As a squire of Stratford, he took more visible pride in his wealth and rank than in his writings. The theater had been the vehicle for his ascent to respect and status. Like a tailor, weaver, or cabinet maker, he had developed and perfected his skills. He saw himself as a craftsman who took pride in his calling. Indeed, in his plays the miller, blacksmith, and weaver are honest tradesmen, treated with a respect he does not extend to the two-faced courtiers in the royal court.

Though the term did not emerge until the end of the century, in effect Shakespeare was a Tory, respecting the artisan more than the entrepreneur and relishing the country more than the city. Shakespeare, who had taken delight in depicting the lives of Plantagenet kings, had an old-fashioned feudal, more than modern Renaissance, philosophy.

Though he must have missed the fellowship of his theatrical colleagues, such as Richard Burbage, John Heminges, and Henry Condell, he did not miss the periphery of court life.

For the King's Men, the principal provider of dramatic material was no longer Shakespeare. Beaumont and Fletcher had taken up the slack, spinning out comedies about the courtly class who now patronized the Globe and Blackfriars theaters.[1]

This playwriting pair, who tried to fill the vacuum left by Shakespeare's retirement to Stratford, had great respect for the Shakespearean magic. Beaumont would write to Ben Jonson in 1610, saying in effect that even though Shakespeare had no university education, he still wrote rings around his contemporaries. This praise of Shakespeare by a contemporary rival is unassailable proof of Shakespeare's authorship, as well as his genius.

> Here I would let slip
> (If I had any in me) scholarship
> And from all learning keep these lines clear
> As Shakespeare's best are, which our heirs shall hear.[2]

Francis Beaumont, who attended Oxford, was the son of a barrister, and John Fletcher, who attended Cambridge, was the son of a bishop. Such were the major distinctions between these two dramatists, who in London shared the same house and the same mistress. In theatrical history their names are forever linked together, just as are the names of Gilbert and Sullivan, and Rodgers and Hammerstein.[3]

In 1613 the bachelor Beaumont married, retired, and died three years later. His former partner Fletcher was approached by the King's Men to write a play about Henry VIII. Yet the best playwright to author a chronicle about the Tudor king was the dramatist who had virtually invented the chronicle play some two decades before. For Shakespeare the request must have been too challenging to reject outright. After all, he could now end his career as he began, with a historical play. At the same time he could close his series of royal portraits, beginning with John in the thirteenth century and ending with Henry VIII in the sixteenth century.

Yet it was not only Fletcher and the King's Men who were pleading with Shakespeare to break his retirement to write a play about Henry VIII. The Earl of Arundel was anxious to redeem his family's name, which had been besmirched by the Tudors. It has been written that Arundel had come to the King's Men offering to underwrite the costs of such a costly chronicle, if they would write and stage it. If he did, the earl commissioned the King's Men to put on *Henry VIII*.[4]

Thomas Howard, the Earl of Arundel, was the head of England's oldest noble family. His grandfather, the Duke of Norfolk, had been executed by Queen Elizabeth in 1572. At the time Norfolk was the last and only duke in England. (Today the Duke of Norfolk is still the premier duke in Britain, and accordingly is the grand marshal of every coronation.) Howard had witnessed his grandfather being beheaded, and then his own father Philip died a prisoner in the Tower. Although Howard inherited the earldom of Arundel from his mother, he was still the first earl in England and one of the wealthiest lords.

Shakespeare had sympathies with the old feudal families, whose rank and power had been debased by Henry VIII and his daughter Elizabeth. As he had once supported Essex, he now was ready to help the Earl of Arundel reclaim his dukedom and the office of Marshal. In *Henry VIII*, Shakespeare wrote a political play.[5] (If he collaborated with Fletcher, the extent of Fletcher's contribution is by no means clear, although a close examination of the material and style lends credence to his involvement.)

Henry VIII was the first English ruler who can be characterized as a Renaissance figure. For all his bluff manners and crude appetites, in his younger days he was everything a complete Renaissance gentleman yearned to be—soldier, sportsman, and somewhat of a scholar. As the King he led troops to Scotland and France. He was a superb horseman, a powerful wrestler, and a proficient player at court tennis. Yet he also had a poetic side; his song "Greensleeves" is still heard today. Like Shakespeare's Falstaff, Henry VIII, despite his vices or because of them, is viewed almost affectionately today. His colorful personality makes him one of the best known of English rulers. Henry VIII, however, was no hero to Shakespeare. Instead, he was the Neronian tyrant who had executed Shakespeare's hero, Sir Thomas More. Early in his career, he had collaborated on a drama about More, but had been stopped by court censors.

The Stuart King James also had his reasons to discourage an unvarnished account of the Tudor Henry VIII, so Shakespeare knew he had to be careful in his treatment of Henry. To put into his mouth the rantings of a despot, as he did with Richard III or Aaron the Moor, would have been imprudent. Time had smoothed the rough edges of the Henry portrait. His divorce of the English Church from Rome—his most remembered act— was a popular decision with rank-and-file Englishmen, whose hated enemy was still Catholic Spain. He was also the father of the late departed Elizabeth, whose robust reign seemed more glorious each year, in contrast with that of the effete James.

The gain in popularity of the Tudor house worried James, and Shakespeare hoped that his chronicle about Henry would tighten the hold of the Stuarts.[6] James Stuart traced his descent not through Henry VIII, but from the father, Henry VII. A play that cast Henry VIII as a royal version of Bluebeard might weaken any remaining Tudor claims to the English throne.

The original title, *All Is True*, suggests that *Henry VIII* is a propaganda play. Yet the chronicle is more of a pageant than a play. If by current comparisons Shakespeare's *Titus Andronicus* was a Stephen King "chiller," *Henry VIII* was more a Cecil B. De Mille spectacular.

In the scene that depicts the coronation of Anne Boleyn, the audience saw earls, dukes, bishops, and judges clothed in exact replicas of the real robes of office, correct down to the last coronet and insignia. The cost of the jewels and embroidered finery ran into thousands of pounds, which by today's reckoning would be millions of dollars.[7] Of course, the colossal production would have been helped by the largesse of the Earl of Arundel.

The era of Henry VIII did not offer the dramatic conflict of either a civil war or a struggle for succession. Shakespeare instead concentrated drawing parallels in the falls of great personages: the Duke of Buckingham, Cardinal Wolsey, and Queen Katherine. To make up for the lack of the swordplay he had once staged to titillate the penny public, Shakespeare substituted the musical pomp of drums and trumpets.

The play begins with a personal note that is as much a disclaimer as it is a description of the play to follow. A commentator in the prologue says on behalf of the playwright:

> I come no more to make you laugh; things now,
> That bear a weighty and a serious brow,
> Sad, high and working, full of state and woe,
> Such noble scenes as draw the eye to flow,
> We now present.

Then, as if to give form to these words, the first act ends with the execution of Buckingham. As Buckingham is sent to the chopping block for getting in the way of Wolsey, he consoles his friends:

> Go with me, like good angels to my end
> And as the long divorce of steel falls on me
> Make of your prayers, one sweet sacrifice
> And lift my soul to heaven.

Queen Katherine receives news of her divorce by Henry. With dignity she sends her best wishes to her former husband:

> Remember me
> In all humility unto his highness:
> Say his long trouble now is passing
> Out of this world.

Cardinal Wolsey is dismissed by the King; yet like Buckingham and Katherine, he offers no word of criticism of Henry.

> If I had but served my God with half the zeal
> I served my king, He would not in mine age
> Have left me naked to mine enemies.

If the play lacks a plot, Shakespeare compensates by serving up rich portraits of those abused by the bloated lusts of a tyrant, such as the betrayed Buckingham, the suffering Katherine, and the faithful Wolsey. Each chooses not to speak out against the king he or she loved and served. Their very silence, however, makes their indictment against their king more eloquent. Shakespeare lets their nobility of conduct speak volumes against the baseness of Henry.

Through Wolsey, Shakespeare in a sense delivers another valedictory. If this is Shakespeare's farewell speech, it is more than just a farewell to theater.

> Farewell! a long farewell, to all my greatness!
> This is the state of man: today he puts forth
> The tender leaves of hopes; tomorrow blossoms,
> And bears his blushing honours thick upon him;
> The third day comes a frost, a killing frost,
> And, when he thinks, good easy man, full surely
> His greatness is a-ripening, nips his root,
> And then he falls, as I do.

In this play, the last that he would ever write or direct, one can imagine Shakespeare attending to every detail: supervising the execution and coronation scenes, checking the robes and regalia of each lord and baronet, renting the jewels, and hiring the trumpeters.

As to that last detail, Shakespeare should have left well enough alone. As the play was staged at the Globe on June 13, 1613, at the last minute he decided to substitute a real cannon for a trumpet, to salute the monarch. Unfortunately, sparks from the cannon blast ignited the thatched roof. The old timbers of the Globe caught fire, and soon the theater was a cauldron. Although there were only two narrow exit doors, a full house escaped unharmed.[8] Sir Henry Wooton, a diplomat who attended, reported that one fleeing theatergoer doused his burning breeches with his pocket flask of beer.[9]

A popular balladeer was singing a song to a lute the following week in London's streets.

Out ran the knights
Out ran the lords
And there was great ado
Some lost their swords
Some lost their hats
Out ran Burbage, too.[10]

Escaping with Richard Burbage was Shakespeare.

As the theater that had premiered his *Hamlet* and *Macbeth* turned to ashes, Shakespeare was shattered. He took steps to sell the London house he had purchased so as to ready the *Henry VIII* performance, and he returned to New Place.[11]

NOTES

1. Marquette Shute, *Shakespeare of London* (New York: Dutton, 1949), pp. 303–4.

2. Tucker Brooke, *Shakespeare of Stratford* (New Haven, Conn.: Yale University Press, 1926), p. 64. The verse is from a verse letter of the dramatist Beaumont to Ben Jonson. It was first printed by W.G.P. in the *Times Literary Supplement*, September 15, 1921, from an old commonplace book. The letter is signed F. B. and is not dated. It may be coeval with some well-known verses of Beaumont to Jonson that are assigned to the period 1608–10.

3. Joseph Quincy Adams, *A Life of William Shakespeare* (Boston: Houghton Mifflin, 1923), pp. 409–10.

4. Peter Levi, *The Life and Times of William Shakespeare* (New York: Holt, 1988), p. 316.

5. Ibid., p. 317.

6. Clara Longworth de Chambrun, *Shakespeare: A Portrait Restored* (London: Holis & Carter, 1957), p. 354.

7. Shute, *Shakespeare of London*, pp. 309–10.

8. Peter Quennell, *Shakespeare: The Poet and His Background* (Cleveland: World, 1963), pp. 321–22.

9. Sir Henry Wooton, *Reliquae Wootonia* (London, 1672), p. 425.

10. "Sonnet on the Pitiful Burning Down of the Globe Playhouse in London," printed in *Gentlemen's Magazine*. It is the same as the "Doleful Ballad" entered in the Stationer's Register in 1613. The manuscript version lies in the collection of John Hopkinson (1610–80), now in the Yorkshire County Archives in Bradford. It was reprinted again in the *Times Literary Supplement* on June 20, 1986.

11. Shute, *Shakespeare of London*, pp. 310–11.

CHAPTER TWENTY-FIVE

Property and Posterity

I make my will then, as sick men do

Pericles
act 1, scene 1

When the Globe celebrated its reopening on March 14, 1614, Shakespeare was persuaded to make one last trip to London. For one thing, he could attend to the settlement and sale of the house he had bought in Blackfriars, both as an investment and as a home during the staging of *Henry VIII*. In addition, his lawyer, Thomas Greene, wanted his famous friend to appear in Chancery to testify against the closing off of certain public lands in Stratford. This was a matter of heated controversy in Warwickshire, and Shakespeare, even if he had a financial interest, was probably reluctant to be involved, but Greene appealed to Shakespeare, as a leading squire of Stratford, to add his distinguished name to the opposition side.[1]

At least outwardly, the life of Shakespeare was a typical success story. A young man born and bred in the country arrives in London poor and gradually makes his fortune there. While amassing his estate, he picks out a country property and lays out his money to purchase it, makes his father a gentleman, and then retires to be a country squire himself.

As Shakespeare mounted his horse in London for the three-day journey back to Stratford, he must have known he was leaving the city for the last time. His regrets were few. He had never liked London, and the sycophantic court of King James had dashed his one-time hopes for the Stuart monarch.

Shakespeare no doubt looked forward to the ride back. He enjoyed horses. With his poetic pen, he had sketched portraits of Antony's horse Adonis; Richard II's roan Barbary; and Petruchio's nag in *Taming of the Shrew*, which suffered from every blemish known to veterinary science.

For Shakespeare the most interesting part would be the last leg of the journey, from Grendon in Buckinghamshire to Stratford through the rolling, sheep-grazing Cotswolds countryside, over a road for which he had only recently supported an appropriation to improve it.[2] Yet the overland 60-mile trek would have taken a toll on his spent frame. He had now passed the half-century mark. By today's standards, one who is just past 50 is still in one's prime, but Shakespeare, who came from a short-lived family, knew that his life was running out.

Shakespeare was the last surviving male in his family. One brother, Richard, had died in his teens. The youngest had been the actor Edmond, whom Shakespeare had buried in a chapel in the Southwark section of London in 1607. And only months before Shakespeare's journey, Gilbert, the last remaining brother, had died.[3]

Shakespeare sensed that something more than age had invaded his body. Scholars today think that he might have contracted Bright's Disease,[4] which attacks the kidneys and saps the strength. Four years before, when he left London for Stratford, he had come home to retire. Now he was returning to die.

Ever sanguine, Shakespeare probably did not spend much time dwelling on the down side of his life—the loss of his son and possibly the death of Essex—but neither was he toting up with pride the many plays with which he had captured London's heart. What occupied his mind was not plays, but property. For Shakespeare, writing had been a rewarding and productive trade, yet he viewed not his literature, but his land as the proof of his success.

The son of an illiterate shopkeeper, Shakespeare had fulfilled his father's dream. He had become a squire with rank and prominence in his native shire. If the pride he took in maintaining his estate and securing its title reflects a proprietary eye, his concern was rooted in an impulse more romantic than materialistic.

Rank not riches had stirred his drive and dreams. Perhaps he still entertained hopes for knighthood and honors. He would receive neither—though long after Shakespeare's death his son-in-law, Doctor Hall, would be offered the former by Charles I in a belated tribute to his Shakespeare connection; even later his godson William D'Avenant would be named poet laureate by Charles II.[5]

As he often revealed in his verse, Shakespeare was matter-of-fact about his mortality. If he thought of posterity, it was limited to property. He had the country squire's desire to ensure that his estate passed down undivided to succeeding generations. Problems, however, clouded the passing of his house and property. They were a feeble wife and a feckless daughter.

For years he had put his pen to the affairs of kings and humankind, but now he turned his flagging energies to personal matters. The solution, he reasoned, was to bequeath his manorhouse to the only capable member of the family—his daughter Susanna.

Today visitors to the clerk's office in Stratford cluck their tongues that Shakespeare only left his wife the second-best bed. Yet Shakespeare knew that the dower rights of common law would automatically award his wife one-third of his estate. He also realized that if he left Susanna the New Place manor, he could be sure that his bedridden wife, who was eight years older, would be cared for by Susanna and Susanna's husband, Doctor Hall, a physician.[6]

As for the number-two bed, that was the bed Anne Shakespeare was already occupying and sharing with her husband. Shakespeare's "best" bed was a formal bedstead used only by visitors in the New Place guest room.[7]

Back in Stratford, Shakespeare did not rush to put his thoughts into legal form. He thought he had time. Whatever was the matter with him physically was more fatiguing than imminently fatal. A horse that has won a race does not immediately come to a standstill, but slowly winds down into a trot that ends in a walk, all the time savoring its triumph. In the same way, Shakespeare now had time to enjoy his family and his friends.

Shakespeare did not let somber thoughts about the legalities of "descent and distribution" dampen his habitual conviviality. As his earliest biographer Nicholas Rowe would write less than a century later, "his pleasurable wit and good nature engaged him in the acquaintance and friendship of [all] the gentlemen in the neighborhood."[8] One of those was Michael Drayton, a fellow Warwickshire poet and royal grammar school classmate with whom he often talked about writing poetry and plays. Drayton's verse, such as "The Ballad of Agincourt," is still quoted.

But most of the time Shakespeare spent with such friends as Hamnet and Judith Sadler, the godparents of his twins; Alderman John Rogers and his son-in-law Robert Harvard (whose son would found the American college); as well as Thomas Greene, whom he often addressed as "cousin." Greene, it will be recalled, had leased New Place when Shakespeare first bought it.

Although generally temperate in his habits, Shakespeare could enjoy an evening over a bottle with friends. In the summer of 1613 he entertained a visiting parson, and a vintner's bill for a bottle of claret and a bottle of sherry is testament to the night's talk about theology and theater.[9]

Occasionally Shakespeare would stop in at his early home on Henley Street, where his favorite sister Joan still lived with her husband William Hart, a hatmaker. (In his will Shakespeare would leave his wardrobe to Joan. Years later a grandchild of Joan Hart would talk about the fun he and his friends had had, playing kings in some of Shakespeare's dusty old theatrical costumes.)[10]

The happiest times, though, were when his daughter Susanna visited New Place with Shakespeare's only grandchild, Elizabeth. Susanna and John Hall were the center of a lively, bright younger set in Stratford. Both were Puritan in their sympathies, but it must be remembered that many Puritans were intellectuals, like the poet Milton, who would champion individual rights and challenge such establishment beliefs as the divine right of kings. Susanna, though her Puritan beliefs might have occasioned some good-natured argument, was a lively and stimulating companion for her father. After Susanna's death in 1649, it would be said that she had received "her intelligence from her father and her character from her Holy Father."[11]

Though Susanna was a delight, the younger one, Judith, was a disappointment.[12] Because her mother was bedridden, as Judith neared 30 she was still unmarried and lived at home. Judith could have assumed more of a role as hostess of New Place, but her failure to ever learn to read or write would not have enhanced that role.

In the last months of 1613, Judith, repeating the history of her mother, became attached to a younger man. This was Thomas Quiney, five years her junior, who ran a tavern in Stratford called the Cave and had developed a reputation that gave little to recommend him as a prospective husband.[13]

Actually, Quiney came from a highly respected local family. His father had followed John Shakespeare as high bailiff of Stratford, and his brother, who had graduated from Oxford with honors, served as a local schoolmaster. Indeed, for three generations the Quineys and Shakespeares had enjoyed intimate ties. Yet the relationship of Thomas with Judith would cool that friendship.

Whether from concern about his younger daughter or because of the advance of his disease, Shakespeare sent for his friend Francis Collins to write a draft of his will in January 1616. Collins, who like Drayton was a comrade from Stratford days, had been recently appointed the Stratford town clerk. According to Stratford tradition, Collins had represented

Shakespeare before Sir Thomas Lucy in the poaching incident of his youth.[14] Collins's draft opened with the traditional Protestant boilerplate of the day:

In the Name of God Amen, I William Shakespeare of Stratford upon Avon on the countie Warr gent in perfect health and memorie God be praysed do make and ordayne this my last will and testament. . . . The matter form following that is to say First I Comend my soule into the hands of God my creator, hoping assuredlie beleeving through the onlie merittes of Jesus Christe.[15]

The will reflected one dominant purpose: to achieve a squire's desire of creating a landed family, leaving the estate intact to a single male descendant where one existed by the means of primogeniture, thereby establishing the Shakespeare family in perpetuity among the landed gentry of Warwickshire.[16]

Accordingly, the estate would descend first to the issue of Susanna. Upon the failure of that line, it would pass to the issue of Judith. Upon the extinction of that branch, the next heir would come from the offspring of his sister, Joan Hart. (In each case, in keeping with the laws of primogeniture, the descent would go to the first son, and in the absence of a son to the eldest daughter.)

The most careful legal draftsman cannot shape destiny. New Place would not even remain in the hands of Shakespeare's heirs through the seventeenth century. Elizabeth Hall, who married the son of the poet Thomas Nashe, and following his death John Barnard, died childless in 1670, by which time the other branches were also extinct.

Yet the royalist Shakespeare would have been proud that New Place would be for three days the home of Queen Henrietta Maria, in July 1643, during the Civil War. The Queen held court in the Shakespeare manor when she joined the troops of her son, Prince Rupert, at Stratford.[17]

So in the will Collins drafted, the legatee of New Place would be, first, Susanna. The only bequests to her sister Judith were the silver plate service and a prized "large gilt silver bowl." An additional £50 was to be granted her if she would waive all rights to the Stratford property in favor of her sister Susanna. The short-changing of Judith was a reflection of his doubts about the prospects of the Quiney relationship and eventual marriage. In the Hall family's possession, New Place would be safe from Quiney's shifty ways.

More interesting than Shakespeare's will were the words he carved out on the flagstone plate covering his future burial place, in the chancel in Holy Trinity Church:

> Good friend for Jesus' sake forbear
> To dig the dust enclosed heare
> Blest be the man that spares these stones
> And curst be he that moves my bones.

Not for Shakespeare was a niche in Westminster Abbey! No move would be made to move his bones. (In *Hamlet*, Shakespeare expresses his horror of disinterment when the Prince finds the skull of Yorick.) Shakespeare, like Churchill centuries later, wanted to be buried in the parish church with his parents—so neither of the two greatest Englishmen would be buried in Westminster Abbey.

Shakespeare was not just a lay reader in the church; he was a lay rector. Part of that honor came from his regular tithing as a communicant, but it was also a testament to his character and his respect in the community. He invoked his rectorial privilege to be buried in the chancel of the church he loved.

Shakespeare was a devout Anglican. He was too much of a patriot to be a "papist" and too much of a ritualist to be a reformer of the liturgy. In an age when men showed little tolerance for faiths other than their own, Shakespeare was broadminded. He sympathized with dispossessed Catholics, and he respected the Puritans—after all, his favorite daughter was a Puritan. He did not discriminate against Jews; in *The Merchant of Venice* and *Othello* he could treat fairly those of the Jewish and Islamic faiths.

Yet his lack of bigotry should not be interpreted as a lack of conviction. His plays ring with references to scripture, much of which he knew from memory. It is even conjectured that he had a hand in the King James version of the Bible. King James authorized the version with his name to replace the sixteenth-century Geneva Bible. This scholarly undertaking produced the first Protestant Bible to be translated directly from the original Hebrew and Greek. Shakespeare was the country's most celebrated poet, and as a gentleman of the bed chamber in King James's court, he would have been a natural choice to smoothe the rough translations of Hebrew poetry, such as the Psalms. Some point to the Psalm 46 in the King James version as bearing a Shakespeare "signature," one of the cryptic codes that were the literary fashion of the day.

Shakespeare was age 46 in 1611, at the date of issue of the King James version. The 46th word from the top in the 46th Psalm is "Shake" ("The earth doth *shake*."), and the 46th word from the bottom is "spear" ("God cutteth forth a *spear*).

The King James Bible and a copy of Shakespeare's works were the two books pilgrims and immigrants from the British Isles would be taking with them to the New World. Both would echo with the Elizabethan majesty of language that Shakespeare perfected and embodied.

NOTES

1. Marquette Shute, *Shakespeare of London* (New York: Dutton, 1949), p. 312.

2. Clara Longworth de Chambrun, *Shakespeare: A Portrait Restored* (London: Holis & Carter, 1957), p. 267.

3. Levi Fox, *The Shakespeare Handbook* (Boston: G. K. Hall, 1987), p. 28.

4. Joseph Quincy Adams, *A Life of William Shakespeare* (Boston: Houghton Mifflin, 1923), p. 460.

5. Chambrun, *Shakespeare: Portrait*, p. 375.

6. Fox, *Shakespeare Handbook*, p. 50.

7. Chambrun, *Shakespeare: Portrait*, p. 372.

8. Nicholas Rowe, *Some Account of the Life etc. of William Shakespeare* (1709).

9. Shute, *Shakespeare of London*, p. 298.

10. Longworth de Chambrun, *Shakespeare: Portrait*, p. 371.

11. Peter Quennell, *Shakespeare: The Poet and His Background* (Cleveland: World, 1963), p. 321.

12. Adams, *Life of Shakespeare*, p. 445.

13. S. Schoenbaum, *William Shakespeare* (New York: Oxford University Press, 1987), pp. 292–96.

14. Chambrun, *Shakespeare: Portrait*, p. 370.

15. Quoted in Schoenbaum, *William Shakespeare*, p. 298.

16. Shute, *Shakespeare of London*, p. 366.

17. Schoenbaum, *William Shakespeare*, p. 305.

Conclusion: Death and Destiny

Their going hence, even as their coming hither.
Ripeness is all.

King Lear
act 5, scene 2

The marriage that Shakespeare hoped would never materialize took place on February 10, 1616. Judith Shakespeare, against her father's wishes, married Thomas Quiney.[1] The ceremony was not an occasion for celebration. Like her parents' marriage 34 years before, it was a hurry-up job. To marry in the pre-Easter season required permission from the Bishop, but neither Shakespeare nor his daughter applied for the license. The resultant fine was a symbolic as well as substantive blot on the marital escutcheon. Yet the heaviest cost of this proscribed lenten marriage was excommunication for the newlyweds.[2]

The sour beginning did not bode a sanguine future for the union. Quiney had insisted on a quick marriage. A Margaret Wheeler claimed she was pregnant with Quiney's child, and Quiney wanted to marry Judith before he was forced to wed the Wheeler girl or, more likely, before Judith's father learned about the affair.[3]

A month later, Shakespeare would read about Quiney's arrest for disorderly conduct in his own establishment, called the Cave. (The phrase "disorderly conduct" was often employed to describe the presence of prostitutes plying their trade.) Quiney was arrested for fornication in

March and soon after was involved in another paternity suit. Yet with all his womanizing, Quiney seems to have had some rough and roguish charm. Certainly, being host of an inn required some measure of affability and good humor. Quiney must also have had some education, since he spoke French. Whatever schooling he had, however, he lacked the ambition to do anything with it. He was content to run an alehouse, sell wine, and take advantage of his connection with the richest men in Stratford.

Still, the marriage, despite Shakespeare's fears, would last. In 1662, Judith would die before her husband. She loved Quiney to the end, even though her steadfast affection was rewarded by frequent infidelity and occasional drunken violence.[4]

Perhaps Judith saw in Thomas Quiney her last chance for marriage and family. At age 31, she must have been tired of spinsterhood and of playing nurse to her bedridden mother. A portrait of Judith made sometime after the marriage shows a feminine but coarser version of her father. She bears his high forehead, hazel eyes, and fair complexion.[5]

Judith's marriage was a further blow to the failing health of Shakespeare. He could no longer put off the signing of his will. Two weeks after his daughter's marriage, he called his lawyer Francis Collins to the home and finally signed the will he had ordered drafted in January. Once Shakespeare had attended to his legal responsibility, he could try to look ahead to happier things.

Ben Jonson, on his way to Scotland for a walking tour, may have written to say he intended to stop in Stratford for a visit.[6] Despite their different theories about theater, Jonson loved his old rival. If he sometimes questioned Shakespeare's scholarship, he had no doubts about his friend's genius. Jonson and Shakespeare must have known that they might be seeing each other for the last time. It is not surprising that Shakespeare could have left his bed for a night out.[7] This recalls Shakespeare's words in *Antony and Cleopatra*,

> Let's have one other gaudy night; call to me
> All my sea captains; fill our bowls once more.

Shakespeare's childhood friend from Warwickshire, Michael Drayton, would join his fellow poets at the reunion. In all likelihood they went to the Cave, Shakespeare's son-in-law's inn, where his daughter now lived. The Cave was situated on the corner of High and Bridge Streets, near Market Cross.

After a meal, which is likely to have been of game, the early supper turned into a nightlong celebration, with many bottles of claret emptied.

The Rev. John Ward reported in his diary, "Shakespeare, Drayton and Jonson had a merry evening and it seems drank too hard."[8]

Jonson might have at first been inhibited by the weakened state of his old friend, but after hours of wine-colored recollections and toasts to past triumphs, Jonson probably began to revert to his old boisterous self. Their rivalry no doubt emerged, with some good-natured taunts and gibes. If so, the modest and retiring Drayton would have been a settling presence.

The reunion with Jonson may have been a tonic for Shakespeare's spirits, but not for his body. He retired to New Place, never again to emerge from his bed. Ward wrote that a heavy fever had followed his evening frolic.

On March 25 Shakespeare sent for Francis Collins to come to his home. Shakespeare wanted to make some alterations to the will he had signed a month before, but he was physically too weak to draft a new will. One change he did make was his leaving his silver-plate service to his grand-daughter, Elizabeth Hall, instead of to Judith. Judith, however, would still receive the "large gilt silver bowl."

Shakespeare left something for the poor of Stratford, but the most interesting bequests were some pounds sterling to be dispensed to Richard Burbage, John Heminges, and Henry Condell to buy remembrance rings.[9] They were the last surviving members of the old Burbage theater troupe that had become the King's Men.

The document was witnessed by his childhood friend Hamnet Sadler, the godfather of his dead son. The shaky inscription of the testator's name on each of the three pages indicates a failing body. Shakespeare was dying, and an elixir of violets recommended by Doctor Hall may have worsened his kidney condition. Hall, in his diary, had reported success with such a potion while administering to Shakespeare's friend Drayton, suffering from a fever only months before.[10]

On April 23, 1616, the town bell of Stratford Chapel rang.[11] The bell ringer was not sounding the tidings of St. George's feast day, but that Stratford's most famous son had died. It is somehow appropriate that the patron saint of the English language would be born and die on the day of the patron saint of England.

Two days later Shakespeare was laid to rest just behind the north wall of the chancel. His daughter Susanna ordered an elaborate monument in marble erected against the wall. Between two marble columns there is a half-length statue of the poet holding pen and paper. A painter was engaged to make a likeness. Shakespeare's eyes are hazel and his hair auburn. The loose gown he wears is black, and the doublet within is the crimson of a former gentleman of the bed chamber to King James. His hands rest on a red and green cushion with gilt tassels. The memorial was a mistake. The intent was no doubt loving, but the result is unworthy. Shakespeare looks like a smug and prosperous burgher.

Stratford had failed in its memorial to Shakespeare, but London did better. During his theatrical career, Shakespeare had never concerned himself with the security of his scripts. They belonged to the company, not to him. Plays were far less valuable than property. But his fellow actors thought otherwise, and they began to assemble their own kind of monument.

Shakespeare's three closest colleagues in the theater were the ring recipients, Burbage, Heminges, and Condell. Burbage did not wear the ring for long; he died in 1619. To the other two fell the task of tracking down the play scripts, which they did with the same love that made them willing to care for the orphaned children of their fellow actors.

In the Epistle Dedicatory to the First Folio, Heminges and Condell write:

We have but collected them and done an office to the dead, to procure his orphans guardians; without ambition either of self-profit or fame; only to keep the memory of so worthy a friend and fellow alive as was our Shakespeare.[12]

No better men could have been found to be the guardians of Shakespeare's "children," for Heminges and Condell were as familiar with Shakespeare's scripts as they could have been with their own families.

The endeavor was both difficult and expensive. The King's Men had on hand some scripts of Shakespeare's more recent plays, but the earlier plays had to be tracked down. Still, when compared with the task of editing, collecting was the easy part.

Old scripts had been published in a "quarto" format, and some of the more popular plays, such as *Titus Andronicus*, *Henry V*, and *Richard III* had been reprinted in several editions. Each edition had compounded the errors of earlier printings, with whole lines, as well as words, omitted, repeated, or garbled. Only Condell and Heminges, two veteran actors whose years on stage had ingrained their minds with the ring of all Shakespeare's lines, could have spotted the egregious errors.[13] The undertaking by Condell and Heminges was a labor of love.

To publish was costly not only in time but in money. Likely purchasers of a Shakespeare folio would be the well-to-do of London, yet Ben Jonson, who was the preferred playwright in intellectual circles, had barely met expenses when he had published a folio of his plays. Plays were not considered worthy of scholarly pursuit. The only possible market was rich theater devotees who wanted a remembrance of the master. As it turned out, however, that proved more than sufficient. The publication of the Folio, in 1623, turned a healthy profit.

But for the efforts of Heminges and Condell, Shakespeare might never have become the major force in the English language. A generation after Shakespeare's death, Cromwell's Protectorate banished the theater, and without the folio, most of the Shakespeare plays would not have survived the Puritan revolution.

Through the succeeding centuries the magic of Shakespeare, instead of fading, has flourished. His poetry permeates the English language, and his characters pervade our literary and political psychology. Today in New York, Shakespeare is the only playwright in the world who may have three or four plays being staged simultaneously. Shakespeare not only outdraws any playwright in New York, London, and the other cities of the English-speaking world, including such far-flung places as Sydney and Bombay, but he also is featured in Moscow, Rome, and Tokyo.

Shakespeare is not only the supreme playwright in the world but the dominant artist. In music, for example, nothing surpasses the influence of his works. His themes have inspired scores of artists in ballet and opera, such as Berlioz, Gounod, Mendelssohn, Verdi, Schubert, and Prokofiev.

As we track his work through the ardent patriotism in his chronicles, the youthful passion of his sonnets, the brilliant sunshine of his comedies, the whirlwind of passions in his tragedies, and the lovely sunset of his final plays, we see that the world is in his debt.

Yet for all his genius, Shakespeare the man was unpretentious. His contemporaries found the Stratford actor a relaxed and amusing companion. Still, he was not the uncomplicated man his congeniality suggests—only the verities he lived by were simple. Though the words sound old-fashioned today, he was a Christian gentleman and a patriot.

Though he was contemptuous both of religiosity and bigotry, Shakespeare knew his Bible and was devoted in his Anglican faith. If he had disdain for Queen Elizabeth, his support of Essex sprang from love of country and a desire to preserve its royal institutions.

He may have wished to be remembered as a Stratford squire and gentleman, but his insights as a poet encompass all humankind. He always mourned the son who was taken from him, but everyone who speaks his language is his heir.

Ben Jonson, in the preface to the Folio published by Heminges and Condell, said it best: "He was not of an age, But for all time! Sweet Swan of Avon!"

NOTES

1. Marquette Shute, *Shakespeare of London* (New York: Dutton, 1949), p. 316.

2. Clara Longworth de Chambrun, *Shakespeare: A Portrait Restored* (London: Holis & Carter, 1957), p. 370; Peter Levi, *The Life and Times of William Shakespeare* (New York: Holt, 1988), p. 338.

3. Ibid., p. 339.

4. Ibid.

5. Chambrun, *Shakespeare: Portrait*, p. 370.

6. Clara Longworth de Chambrun, *Shakespeare: Actor-Poet* (London: Appleton, 1927), p. 246.

7. Chambrun, *Shakespeare: Portrait*, p. 373.

8. Joseph Quincy Adams, *A Life of William Shakespeare* (Boston: Houghton Mifflin, 1923), pp. 460–61; Peter Quennell, *Shakespeare: The Poet and His Background* (Cleveland: World, 1963), p. 333.

9. Shute, *Shakespeare of London*, pp. 318–19.

10. Chambrun, *Shakespeare: Actor-Poet*, p. 246.

11. Shute, *Shakespeare of London*, p. 320.

12. Quoted in Shute, *Shakespeare of London*, pp. 324–25; also see Levi Fox, *The Shakespeare Handbook* (Boston: G. K. Hall, 1987), p. 178.

13. Shute, *Shakespeare of London*, p. 330.

Selected Bibliography

Adams, Joseph Quincy. *A Life of William Shakespeare*. Boston: Houghton Mifflin, 1923.
Aubrey, John. *Anecdotes and Miscellany*. London: Edward Castle, 1696.
———. *Brief Lives Chiefly of My Contemporaries*. Oxford: J. Johnson, 1927. Bodleian Library, Oxford.
Bakeless, John. *Christopher Marlowe*. New York: William Morrow, 1937.
Brooke, Tucker. *Shakespeare of Stratford*. New Haven, Conn.: Yale University Press, 1926.
Burton, S. H. *Shakespeare's Life and Stage*. Edinburgh: W. & R. Chambers, 1989.
Chambers, E. K. *William Shakespeare*. Oxford: Clarendon Press, 1930.
Chambrun, Clara Longworth de. *Shakespeare: A Portrait Restored*. London: Holis & Carter, 1957.
———. *Shakespeare: Actor-Poet*. London: Appleton, 1927.
Fluchere, Henri. *Shakespeare and the Elizabethans*. New York: Hill & Wang, 1956.
Ford, Boris, ed. *Age of Shakespeare*. New York: Penguin, 1982.
Fox, Levi. *The Shakespeare Handbook*. Boston: G. K. Hall, 1987.
Fuller, Thomas. *The Book of Worthies*. 2 vols. London: J. G., W. L., and W. G., 1662.
Furnivall, F. J., and John Munro. *Shakespeare: Life and Work*. London: Cassel, 1908.
Harbage, Alfred. *Shakespeare's Audience*. New York: Columbia University Press, 1941.
Kennedy, Milton. *The Oration in Shakespeare*. Chapel Hill, N.C.: Chapel Hill Press, 1941.
Levi, Peter. *The Life and Times of William Shakespeare*. New York: Holt, 1988.
Neilson, William, and Ashley Thorndike. *The Facts about Shakespeare*. New York: Macmillan, 1921.
O'Toole, Fantan. *No More Heroes: A Radical Guide to Shakespeare*. Dublin: Raven Arts Press, 1890.
Papp, Joseph, and Elizabeth Kirkland. *Shakespeare Alive*. New York: Viking, 1989.
Quennell, Peter. *Shakespeare: The Poet and His Background*. Cleveland: World, 1963.
Riggs, David. *Ben Jonson*. Cambridge: Harvard University Press, 1989.

Rowe, Nicholas. *Works*. 2 vols. London: J. & R. Tonson, 1770.

Schoenbaum, S. *William Shakespeare*. New York: Oxford University Press, 1987.

Shute, Marquette. *Shakespeare of London*. New York: Dutton, 1949.

Spalding, K. J. *The Philosophy of Shakespeare*. New York: Oxford University Press, 1953.

Van Doren, Mark. *Shakespeare*. New York: Holt, 1939.

Wain, John. *The Living World of Shakespeare*. New York: St. Martin's, 1966.

Walker, Margaret. *Shakespeare without Tears*. New York: Premier, 1964.

Index

ABOUT THE AUTHOR

JAMES C. HUMES is Senior Fellow and Lecturer at the University of Pennsylvania Graduate School—Fels Center of Government. He is an accomplished professional speaker, a speechwriter for three presidents, an actor, a playwright, and an author. Among his books are *My Fellow Americans* (Praeger, 1992), *Churchill, Instant Eloquence, The Sir Winston Method*, and *The Benjamin Franklin Factor*. He was Editorial Advisor for President Ford's memoirs, *A Time to Heal*. He has written and performed two plays, *Blood, Sweat, and Tears* (a one-man Churchill show) produced by PBS in 1985, and *What's Happening at the Convention, Dr. Franklin?* for the U.S. Constitution Bicentennial Commission in 1987.